Richard Glover's skewed s
a world both weird and wry – in which ⌐⌐⌐⌐
provides marriage advice, J.D. Salinger celebrates tap
water and naked French women bring forth a medical
miracle. It's also a world in which shampoo is eschewed,
the second-rate is praised and George Clooney's haircut
can help save a relationship.

Bizarre yet commonplace, absurd yet warm-hearted,
these stories will expose the true strangeness of the life
you are living right now.

*

Richard Glover has written a number of books,
including *In Bed with Jocasta*, *The Dag's Dictionary*,
Desperate Husbands, *The Mud House* and *Why Men
Are Necessary*. He writes a hilarious weekly column for
the *Sydney Morning Herald* and presents *Thank God
It's Friday* on ABC Radio.

To find out more, visit www.richardglover.com.au.

GEORGE CLOONEY'S CLOONEY'S HAIRCUT

and other cries for help

GEORGE CLOONEY'S HAIRCUT

and other cries for help

RICHARD GLOVER

ABC
Books

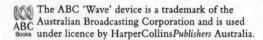 The ABC 'Wave' device is a trademark of the
Australian Broadcasting Corporation and is used
under licence by HarperCollins*Publishers* Australia.

First published in Australia in 2013
by HarperCollins*Publishers* Australia Pty Limited
ABN 36 009 913 517
harpercollins.com.au

HarperCollins*Publishers*
Level 13, 201 Elizabeth Street, Sydney NSW 2000, Australia
Unit D, 63 Apollo Drive, Rosedale, Auckland 0632, New Zealand
A 53, Sector 57, Noida, UP, India
77–85 Fulham Palace Road, London W6 8JB, United Kingdom
2 Bloor Street East, 20th floor, Toronto, Ontario M4W 1A8, Canada
10 East 53rd Street, New York NY 10022, USA

National Library of Australia Cataloguing-in-Publication entry:

Glover, Richard, author.
  George Clooney's haircut and other cries for help / Richard
  Glover.
  978 0 7333 3229 6 (paperback)
  978 1 4607 0030 3 (ebook)
  Australian wit and humor.
  Australia – Social life and customs – Humor.
A828.302

Cover design by Simon Letch
Cover images: Richard Glover by Lisa Tomasetti; George Clooney's haircut by
  Mark Davis; all other images by shutterstock.com
Typeset in Sabon LT by Kirby Jones
Printed and bound in Australia by Griffin Press
The papers used by HarperCollins in the manufacture of this book
are a natural, recyclable product made from wood grown in sustainable
plantation forests. The fibre source and manufacturing processes meet
recognised international environmental standards, and carry certification.

8 7 6 5 4   14 15 16 17

For Fred O'Brien

Contents

Chapter 5

In which the Bible is rewritten by IKEA, Leibniz is put in his place and some French women remove all their clothing

Chapter 6

In which a world record is broken, a literary map is drawn and the niceness epidemic is revealed

Chapter 7

In which the world ends, but not before Paul Keating confronts the day and Hedy Lamarr presents her beauty tips

Chapter 8
In which shampoo is abandoned and an
optimist's errata is compiled

Chapter 1

In which Jocasta racks off
to Melbourne, Henry VIII
provides marriage advice
and Vishnu tries to get
some sleep

The Devolution of Man

Who'd live alone? I know millions do it. Just not me. Not until now. Suddenly Jocasta is perpetually in Melbourne. I imagine she's shacked up with either a crime lord or a wanky theatre director – these two occupations being my only available image of what people do in Melbourne. Our children, having spent the past decade stealing coins off my bedside table, are both on the sort of overseas holiday I would dream of if only someone hadn't stolen all the coins off my bedside table.

So it's me and the dog and what can only be described as a downward trajectory. Here's my question for those millions who manage – nay, enjoy – living on their own: How do you maintain standards? If no one is there to witness that second bowl of ice-cream, or that fifth glass of wine, then has it really happened? Is it like the tree that falls unobserved in the forest?

This is the way I find myself behaving as a single person: a man with no standards, no self-respect, and – crucially – no witnesses.

Most of my good behaviour, I now realise, is an attempt to impress Jocasta and distract her from the less savoury aspects of my character. This is all very well, right up to the moment she goes away.

Robbed of the chance to brag to your partner – 'See, I did all the laundry'; 'The bathroom, you might notice, is spotless'; 'My fungal infection is clearing up' – how do you manage to maintain an interest in such matters? What's to stop the laundry from piling up, together with the household garbage and the unwashed plates and pans, until the neighbours start complaining about the stench, the council whacks a fumigation order on the house and you find yourself the subject of a tabloid current affairs show? 'Strange Hermit Lives with Rats and Mice in Foetid House of Shame' is presumably the headline *A Current Affair* will use to advertise my story.

Certainly, with every night alone, my behaviour worsens. Jocasta, most weeks, flies to Melbourne on Monday morning. Monday night, I'm fine. Home-cooked dinner, two beers, a news show on TV, one chapter of a literary novel and bed. By Tuesday, it's a frozen dinner, five wines, a comedy DVD and a perv at the catalogue for the DJs lingerie sale. Plot this on a chart and you'll see the steepness of the curve. By Friday, I'm pissed at 8.30pm, no dinner, the dog's whining for food, I'm lying on the couch watching the arse-end of my ten-DVD Steve Coogan box-set, finding myself unable to comprehend either my own thoughts or the simplest of Steve's plots. By this point, I've lost the gift of language and am communicating with the dog via a series of grunts and whistles.

Continue this for a few weeks and I doubt I'd be fully human. Evolution itself would be thrown into reverse. Week two and the opposable thumb would go; week three and I'd lose the ability to walk erect. Stay away long enough and I'd probably become aquatic.

Already, the dog and I spend most of our time slinking around on the floor fighting over food scraps. It's like some sort of post-nuclear dystopia. Every time I try to change the DVD, the dog stands in front of the set and growls. It seems he likes Coogan's early material.

The supermarket doesn't help. I go shopping on Sunday afternoon to stock up for the week, and that's when the downward spiral begins. I search for things in packets for one, but the choice is extremely limited. Some packets explicitly say 'serves two'. It's the first time in my life I've been openly mocked by pre-pack meat.

Oh, I know it's possible to buy the two-pack and freeze half, but why should I? It's like a letter of reproach, sitting there in the fridge. Instead, I settle for a pack of smoked salmon, some pasta and a tub of cream; I'll get three dinners out of it. Sure, it's fattening, but who cares? If a man gets fat in the forest and no one sees the outward slump of his belly, has the weight gain really occurred? If he eats takeaway pizza straight from the box, observed only by the dog, is the universe any the wiser?

Presumably this downward trajectory eventually slows; the track of the rollercoaster, I hope, first flattens and then starts to rise as the human urge for self-respect and decency reasserts itself. Half the people I know live alone. They seem perfectly happy. Their houses are tidy; their waistlines reasonable. Their alcoholism seems no more advanced than my own. How do they do it? Can it be that they develop some sort of internal system of standards and hygiene rather than simply forcing their partner into the role of police officer, diet coach and moral arbiter?

Self-regulation. I turn the concept over in my mind and find it quite remarkable.

A few days later, Jocasta limps through the door about midnight, tired and hungry after another week in Melbourne. As usual, the planes were all delayed. If the Americans want to impose a no-fly zone in parts of the Middle East, they should call in the staff of Melbourne airport. They operate one every Friday night.

I have scrubbed the house ready for her arrival, removing all signs of drunkenness and Coogan-watching. I have stashed all the empty wine bottles in the recycling bins of our neighbours. I have removed a week's worth of discarded socks from the floor in front of the couch.

Nothing I can do, however, makes up for the area, nay the city, in which our house is situated.

Jocasta, you understand, is working in Fitzroy, which, on my observation, is groovy to an absurd degree. Peering from a taxi on my first visit, there appeared to be endless kilometres of funky bars, one-off fashion shops and eclectic little art galleries. 'Just how many blocks does the groovy go?' I asked Jocasta but she just gestured out the window airily as if to say: 'Further than you could possibly imagine.'

Certainly, it makes home seem a little bland. As I pour her a drink and watch her play with the dog, I feel a bit defensive about the joint. I think this is a peculiarly Sydney feeling: everyone in the world thinks their own city is terrific except us. Ask most Sydneysiders what they think of their home town and they'll crinkle their nose as if to indicate a whole city that has just trodden in dog shit. We think it's overcrowded. We think it's overpriced. In our honest moments, we think it's a bit bogan. In Melbourne, the phrase 'a splash of colour' means a whip-thin girl with pink hair and a little black dress; in Sydney, it means a footballer vomiting onto the Corso.

'Some dinner?' I ask as Jocasta sits down to open her mail. She says yes, which surprises me, given the lateness of the hour. I find myself thinking: 'This eating at midnight, it must be a Melbourne thing.'

How can I ever make our small part of Sydney measure up to her weekday slice of Melbourne? I contemplate opening a funky cocktail bar in the shed up the back, or redecorating the lounge room with a colourful series of various found objects.

Maybe if I unpacked all our mouldy boxes of old clothes, I could set up a '70s retro shop just like the one I saw in Brunswick Street.

I cook some pasta and serve it with a spoon or two of leftover bolognaise sauce.

'It's good to have a home-cooked meal,' Jocasta says as I place the plate in front of her. She's clearly delusional if she thinks this reheated slop can be dignified as a 'home-cooked meal'. Maybe they're more polite in Melbourne.

More likely she senses my anxiety that I can't measure up. I've seen people in Fitzroy. They are all thin and young and wear black and have good haircuts. I'm old and crotchety and have been so busy watching television I haven't been to the hairdresser for months. Without his ministrations, my eyebrows look like a couple of hairy caterpillars who have died while mating on my forehead. I'm also developing mad hair. In terms of hair, I'm one week off the Unabomber.

What is it about Melbourne? The whole population is twenty-five years old and has money to burn. In Sydney, everyone is fifty-three and skint. Down there, a night out means a $12 glass of Tasmanian pinot in an art-gallery nightclub; up here it means a skinful of Tooheys New followed by a punch-up with Warren the cellarman in the back car park.

I try to think of some good things about my city. The harbour is one of the world's great wonders, so it's hardly surprising they're planning to build a casino that will be visible from every shore. With a bit of creativity, they'll whack a wall between North Head and South Head and concrete the lot. It should be the slogan on our number plates: 'We came, we saw, we concreted'.

There's a rustling from under the sink, indicating the presence of a mouse. A couple of cockroaches are parading on the curtains. I hope Jocasta doesn't notice. It must be quite hard, going from a smart, serviced apartment to what is literally a vermin-infested hovel.

I try to distract her by offering a drink. As it happens, I have a good bottle of Tasmanian pinot.

'A pinot, darling?' I say, trying to make my voice trill in what I imagine is a sophisticated Melbourne way.

'No thanks,' Jocasta replies sweetly, 'I'll just have a Tooheys New. And another spoonful of this inedible slop.'

I serve the beer and she flashes me a winning smile. 'It's good to be home,' she says as she swigs at the bottle. 'They're all up 'emselves in Melbourne.'

Memory Aide

I've been watching the miniseries *The Tudors* and realise I need to live like Henry VIII. Not the six wives, just the retinue. I love the way people are announced as they walk in the door: 'Your Highness – here enters the Duke of Witherspoon.' Or 'May I present the Earl of Curmudgeon?' For a man who can no longer remember anybody's name, this could be a real lifesaver.

I could sit at home on the couch, a liveried flunky standing by the door. 'M'lord, these are your neighbours, Susie and Bill Umbrage, accompanied by their children, Samantha and Peter Umbrage.' Or, perhaps, up at the local shops: 'This is the school principal, Tim Rictus, whom you've known for many years, and his daughter, Ella Rictus-Pyke.'

I walk around the neighbourhood and meet people I've known for years. Rarely can I remember their names. The problem, I fear, is this: when I first meet someone, they tell me their name but, unfortunately – at this very moment – I'm so busy smiling and looking agreeable, I have no time to take in the details. So forever afterwards,

I find their name is missing. You'll spot the implication: smiling and acting as if I am normal is clearly such a stretch, it requires 100 per cent of my concentration. As a result, if I've met you, almost by definition, I have no idea who you are.

Where's that in the list of seven deadly sins? It's not pride or avarice or gluttony. It's a sin called 'being such a strange, anxious person that appearing vaguely human when meeting others involves a big effort'. So why isn't that on the list?

The names of children, in particular, are almost impossible to remember. Jocasta seems able to do it. On Sunday, driving up Epping Road to see friends, I glance at other vehicles and imagine that in each, the same half-whispered conversation is in progress: 'She's called Trish and is a dentist; the husband is Rod and works in shipping; and the children are called Jack and Olivia.'

Like the man in every car, I mouth the names several times in an attempt to fix them in my brain. I'm doomed to failure. Nearly all modern children are called Jack and Olivia – or occasionally William and Chloe – names designed to wriggle free from my memory. Like a stealth bomber, they'll leave no record of their transit across my mind. And so, an hour later, I'll be at some barbecue three suburbs away and Jack-or-is-it-William will be torturing the family cat or drowning in the pool and I'll find myself summoning help with the phrase: 'What's-his-name, um, the small male one, you know, about a metre high ...'

By this point I'll also have forgotten Rod's name, or was it Rob, the one who was in shipping, or was it storage?

None of this goes down well with the hosts, for whom the child is a sun around which all planets orbit. I'll leap into the pool fully clothed to save the little wretch and yet my fumble in the name department will be all that's remembered. Suddenly the cheery offers of 'another glass of chardonnay?' or 'care for another salmon puff' will become 'here's a glass of tap water as you head out the door'.

Too many names crowd in, all demanding our attention. We now, for example, are required to know the name of a pastry chef called Adriano Zumbo, who apparently has been featured on the television program *MasterChef,* and, at the same time, one is supposed to be oh-so-familiar with the Latin dance exercise program Zumba. This is asking too much of those of us over twenty-five.

Inevitably, I find myself around a kitchen table, the tea being poured by my younger son or his delightful girlfriend, the air alive with friendly banter, all happiness and pleasure, at which point I happen to request 'another one of those delicious macarons from Anthony Zumba'.

This causes Jocasta, my son the Space Cadet, and the Space Cadet's girlfriend, to bend double with laughter; laughter that continues for far longer than is charitable. Remarkably, I can also hear the sound of them rolling their eyes, which gives you some indication of how loudly they do it.

Which brings us back to Henry VIII. If I were Henry and had made a similarly tiny error, a fawning courtier would cough discreetly and whisper in my ear: 'I believe Your Highness will find he favours the macarons of Mr Adriano Zumbo, Zumba being an exercise craze currently popular in Your Majesty's kingdom.'

Should laughter none-the-less occur, or even a subtle twitching of the muscles around the mouth, the real Henry VIII would have summoned the Constable of the Tower and all three of his tormentors would have been removed for beheading, their cries for mercy ignored while Henry and the flunky busied themselves finishing off the macarons, which, by the way, are quite spectacular.

In fact, Zumbo himself may well have been summoned and forced to change his name to Zumba, taking upon himself the blame for any regal misunderstanding: 'It was stupid of me, Your Highness, to half-share a name with an exercise craze. I do beg Your Majesty's pardon.'

At this point, Zumba, or is it Zumbo, would throw himself prostrate, or is it prostate, before me, hardly breathing, in his fear.

'Oh, just keep the macarons coming, especially the one with the passionfruit ganache,' I'd say with a royal wave of the hand, further cementing my reputation as a king in whom toughness and benevolence are combined in equal measure.

Certainly, the palace walls would ring with the terrified cries of Jocasta and the young people as they were prepared for execution, their hideous yelps drowned out in my own head by the pleasing crunch of Mr Zumbo's zesty confection.

In truth, I'd probably save Jocasta from the beheading at the last minute. In my ambition to be more like Henry VIII, I believe she could perform the roles of all six wives. When we first met she was a bit Catherine of Aragon, intense and serious; then, in her late twenties, she became witty and saucy like Anne Boleyn; and in her thirties there was a sweetly maternal patch, à la Jane Seymour.

In a few years' time I'd like to see her have a shot at being Catherine Parr, nursing me as I succumb to syphilis and gluttony. At that point, I'll at least be forgiven for not knowing anyone's name. More macarons, anyone?

Second Coming

Suddenly everyone has a problem with people who come second. It has to be gold or nothing. But what's so bad about coming second? Silver, in my mind, is the new gold. I'm thinking of packaging my ideas into a motivational speech. 'Aim high-ish,' I'll tell my corporate clients. 'Try to be pretty much the best person you can be, without busting a boiler.' And, as the closing message of my speech: 'Sometimes near enough *is* good enough.'

Think back to your class at school. Where is the kid that came first? Most of the time he or she went off the rails in the year after school and is now living in a tin shed just outside Darwin, subsisting on a diet of surgical spirits and hydroponic dope. Occasionally he – or she – accepts care parcels from the kid that came second in the class, who now runs most of South-East Asia for a fast-growing internet start-up.

When dating, we all know to avoid the best-looking person in the room. They are vain creatures who think they're doing you a favour by saying hello. They already have a regular lover, one they meet whenever they look into a mirror. The real trick is to nab the silver medallist: attractive enough, yet with sufficiently weird-shaped ears they'll make an effort.

If only I could come second in most things.

I'd like to be the second-fittest person in any session at the gym, the fittest being a strange man with a baby-oil dependency and shrunken testicles due to steroid abuse. He spends half his life at the gym and his chest looks like a plaster cast of Christina Hendricks's bottom.

I'd like to be the second-best employee in my office; the gold medallist being the sap who makes life a misery for everyone else by over-complicating every task and who'll dutifully die from a coronary two days before retirement, thus sparing the firm the $5 cost of a farewell card.

I'd like to be the second-best father in the neighbourhood. The best father – a man who is never tipsy, or crotchety, or tardy in serving his family's every whim – having left his children with quite unreasonable expectations of what life has to offer.

I'd like to be the second-best husband in our street, still spotting the attractive yet age-appropriate woman strolling past as we walk the dog, while also glancing up so surreptitiously that my partner assumes I'm merely assessing the weather or correcting a crick in my neck.

I'd like to pay a silver medallist's level of attention to politics: knowing that it's wrong to be uninterested in the great public debates of our time but also realising that the people who know most about politics are nearly always complete fanatics.

And I'd like to be a silver medallist at healthy and ethical eating, avoiding both the death-by-salt diet of some bloke who only ever eats at Macca's *and* the gold-medal standard represented by the total bore who fusses and frets about every ingestible thing, making himself the mournful centre of attention at each social occasion as the host rushes around, beset by guilt, realising he's forgotten to order the vegan burgers, the GM-free corn chips and the cider brewed from Amazonian bush fruits collected in sustainable forests by local indigenous tribespeople.

'Try to get to the top of the tree,' we're told by the motivational cheer squad, but the top of most trees is an uncomfortable and dangerous spot. The branches are thin and spindly and bend from side to side whenever there's a high wind. A few metres down, there's a much better position: stable, so you can sit a while, and with a view that's just as good. It's the silver medallist's perch and it's always been the best place to survey the world.

The trouble with sport generally – whether it's the Olympics or a local football match – is the claim that it represents more than entertainment and excitement. People talk about sport as if it exists to provide life advice for the rest of us: as you watch you should be inspired to strive for excellence, for a gold medal in your field, just like the athletes on the track.

'Being the best you can be' sounds a good idea but it nearly always involves obsession – sacrificing many things for this one thing.

It's not only swimmers or runners. In her book *Stravinsky's Lunch*, Drusilla Modjeska explains how the composer forced his family to eat every meal in silence lest they derail the great man's train of thought. Maybe those lunches were worth it for Stravinsky; it's less likely they were pleasant for Mrs Stravinsky and the little Stravinskys.

Obsession may work out for the occasional pole-vaulter or sprinter, scientist or artist. Most of us, though, want more from life: we are more ambitious, not less. We want a *pretty* good job; to be *quite* fit and healthy; to be *reasonably* good parents and partners; to have a fair crack at being a good friend, citizen, neighbour, cook, dancer, gardener, joke-teller.

We want it all. To be creative *and* allow our children to speak during lunch, even if it means tiny compromises in just about everything we do. That's the Olympic slogan for the real world: Quite High. Fairly Fast. Reasonably Strong.

Here's wishing you silver in all that you do.

The Vishnu Syndrome

Could someone explain why my body grows an extra arm as soon as I try and go to sleep? When I approach the bed I have only two arms, which hang tidily from my shoulders. Then I climb into the bed, lie on my side and suddenly I have more arms than I can easily handle.

What to do with them? I can crook one of them under my head, jamming the pillow in between, but this makes my head too high, so instead I try stretching the arm out, which brings complaints from the Other Bed User ('Your hand is touching my hair. It feels like spiders are crawling in my hair'). Meanwhile there's another arm with nowhere to go, so I try crooking that up over my head, but that feels weird, then stretching it out ('You're touching my hair again'), then folding it up with the other one, which makes me feel like a school principal speaking sternly at assembly.

By now the pillow has become too warm so I have to flip it over to the cool side and then rearrange my various arms, so numerous I feel I'm Vishnu, the Hindu god. It's at this point my hip starts hurting.

On radio I once had the chance to interview Greg Chamitoff, the NASA astronaut, and he described the process of sleeping in zero gravity. On the International Space Station, there's no contact with the bed. You just hover above it, loosely tethered so you don't drift away. How glorious. Pillow never hot, hip never hurty, and your various arms can just go wherever they please, the floating tentacles of an easy-go-lucky octopus. No wonder so many people dream of being astronauts.

Back on earth, I keep flipping from one side to the other. Each new position feels okay for a moment, then gravity catches on to what I'm doing. It knows to press down on precisely the most uncomfortable bits. I'll have to flip again. Maybe I'd be better on my back? Or chest-down? Or curled up like a ball? ('Could you *please* stop shifting around?') They could print a whole book illustrating the various sleeping positions *Joy of Sex* style: The Passed-out Drunk; The Ball of Wool; The Saturday Night Fever.

I try to distract myself by thinking about something peaceful but my brain won't play along. My brain is firmly anti-sleep. It believes sleep is to be avoided.

Well, I'll just switch off my brain by thinking about lovely butterflies dancing in the air on a hot summer's day. It's been so hot this summer. That much was clear from those terrible bushfires. I hope the house insurance is up to date. Strange, but I can't remember paying it ...

By now the doona is all bunched up on my side ('You've taken all the doona'), so I sit up and use a couple of my arms to rearrange it ('Why are you making such a meal of it?'), at which point I notice that it's past midnight, so I'll have less than six and a half hours' sleep and that's if I FALL ASLEEP RIGHT THIS SECOND.

Alas, that's unlikely to happen since I am now feverishly calculating the hours between this moment and dawn, while becoming increasingly anxious about how wretched I'll feel in the morning.

Oh no. Pillow hot again. Hip sore. Try flipping over to face Other Bed User ('You're touching my hair again'). Maybe it would be better on my back. ('Are you sleeping on your back? You always snore when you sleep on your back.') Okay, I'll sleep on the other side, which means staring right at the alarm clock. Now less than six hours to morning. To be precise: five hours and fifty-five minutes until alarm time.

Five hours fifty-four now.

Five hours fifty-three.

My God the tick-tock is loud.

I might try angling the clock away so I can't see the clock face. ('What are you fidgeting with? Can't you just go to sleep?')

The pillow is too thin, that's the problem. Maybe if I doubled it over. Trouble is, that makes it too thick. What about single thickness but with one of my arms stuck beneath to give it more height? ('What's with all the pillow action? Don't you know what time it is?')

Actually no, because I moved the clock, but it probably would be good to check so I know how tired I'll be.

Very tired. That's how tired. 1.22am. That's – let me count – five hours and eight minutes' sleep, if I went to sleep now, which I can't do because my arm has pins and needles from being bunched beneath my head. But here's an idea: what if I cautiously and very slowly straightened my arm and, yes, crept it into the gap between the top of the mattress and the wall, while being very careful not to touch the hair of the Other Bed User.

Done. Achieved. Bliss at last.

'Arghhh. You're touching my hair. It feels like spiders. Why do you keep touching my hair?'

Am I too old to apply for NASA and be blasted into outer space? Jocasta, I'm sure, would be sure to support my application.

A Dog's Life

My local newspaper has had the chance to use the classic headline: 'Man Bites Dog'. The story was about a wrongdoer who, while being arrested, attempted to bite the police dog. The dog, Dexter, bit him back, executing the bite with somewhat more skill than that exhibited by the man. There was a great quote from the police officer in charge: 'As you can imagine, Dexter did a better job of it.'

At last report, the man was in hospital, being stitched together by doctors.

It was a situation in which the skills of man and those of dog were compared and – this once – the skills of man were found wanting.

It's easy, after all, to list the things humans do better than dogs. Give a dog a mobile phone and he's hard-pressed to use it. Dogs rarely stand for election. As food critics they are often undiscerning: unable, on occasion, even to say whether the meal, though delicious, involved chicken or beef or fish.

And yet. And yet.

A dog is better at biting. A dog is better at sleeping. A dog mostly has good dreams, in which his legs twitch and circle as if he's a young puppy perpetually chasing rabbits beneath an always-blue sky.

A dog makes the best of things. Our dog, Darcy, fed in the late afternoon, drinks heartily from his water bowl at precisely the moment the rest of us sit down to eat our dinner. It's not as good as a second serve of that delicious chicken – or was it beef? – but it joins him to the celebratory mood.

A dog does not judge a book by its cover. A tiny dog, or a large dog, met in the park is treated with the same respect as a dog one's own size. There's no focus on the colour of another's pelt or whether the fur is worn Afro-style, clipped or shaggy. A cheaply made dog collar will never cause the new friendship to falter. A dog is a dog, except perhaps for the occasional Great Dane, which, admittedly, can be a little off-putting. ('I fear someone has mistakenly brought a horse to the park. I find myself, perchance, preferring to walk on the far side.')

A dog can find hours of pleasure snapping his jaws at flies, though nary a one is caught. He enjoys it when the phone rings, although he's as uninterested as the rest of us in the latest deal from Energy Australia. And he loves responding to the doorbell, though it's so rarely for him.

Dogs possess superior creativity. When humans are in control of a household, a rubbish bin is just a rubbish bin. It's a receptacle for rubbish. Place that rubbish bin and its contents under the supervision of a dog –

a task achieved by leaving the house for work – and it's transformed into so much more. A food larder. An entertainment centre. An aromatic on-floor wallowing pond. By late afternoon, it may even be pressed into service as a home decorator's gift shop, its objects distributed and displayed in every room of the house and through much of the garden.

As with all of us, there are imperfections. My own dog has a thing about wheelie bins, which he believes are a malevolent force about to take over the world. He barks and cowers to warn me of the deadly threat, amazed that I am strangely oblivious. I assume he's impressed by my bravery, when, on a regular weekday morning, I manhandle the thing off our property, casting it into the street, the dog mystified when I change my mind that very evening, assisting the hated creature back up the driveway, so it can resume its mission of glowering at him.

In all other ways, he represents the superior species. Only a dog can create a ceremony from the simple act of lying down – elegantly circling the spot before collapsing as if tasered, the thud when hitting the ground so expressive of the state of relaxation that has been instantly achieved. And only a dog can get a thrill from being reunited with a long-lost friend, even though the friend is you and you've been 'long-lost' only in the sense that you disappeared for forty-two seconds while retrieving something from the car. ('You were gone *soooo* long. I missed you *soooo* much. Were you overseas or interstate?')

We humans sit with our problems of self-esteem, not liking to ask for love because we secretly wonder if we deserve it. Not so the dog, secure enough in his self-belief that he'll use his wet nose to forcibly reposition a human hand so it no longer wastes time holding a book, or flicking the pages of a newspaper, or reaching for a cup of tea, but instead fulfils its proper function scratching his head or rubbing his tummy.

We are superior, perhaps, in possessing an opposable thumb. But they are superior in understanding the tasks for which those dexterous human hands should always be used – fetching a dog's bowl, picking up a dog's poo, tickling a dog's ear.

And setting up the rubbish bin for tomorrow's adventures. Maybe Dexter would care to join Darcy for a wallow.

Past Imperfect

In my favourite small town, Taralga, they've done up the top pub. It's all plasma TVs and marble tabletops. There's a wine list and fine food. The place is terrific. Part of me, though, liked the old pub.

Back in the 1990s, I used to go to Taralga all the time, choosing either top pub or bottom pub. The typical scene involved three sheep farmers, all wearing beanies to banish the cold, sitting in steely silence and staring into the middle distance. The only noise was provided by the microwave, which would occasionally go 'ping' to signify the arrival of another meat-pie-in-a-plastic-bag, presented – in a miracle of physics – with burning-hot centre and freezing-cold exterior.

There was also a framed photo of the local footy team and a blackboard with the latest footy results. There were three teams in the competition, so you probably had a fair chance of making the semis.

Conversations were not plentiful, yet I had a beauty with a woman in her eighties who had just moved to town.

'Why have you come to Taralga?' I asked.

'Oh, to die,' she said brightly. 'The local cemetery is quite marvellous.'

She took a sip of her beer and described the scenic qualities of the Stonequarry Cemetery.

'It's up on Golspie Road,' she advised. 'You should take a look. Perfect place for when you're dead.'

I promised I'd check it out.

The conversation fitted the bleak old pub and the dying old town. Now, in the past few years everything has changed. The drought has broken, the countryside is greener, and the town is busier. People move there to live, not die. And the pub has marble tabletops.

Yet, for some of us, there is nostalgia in the ratty, crappy, frayed Australia of a few decades ago: the Australia in which not every sandwich had to feature marinated goat's feta, chargrilled capsicum, and a price tag of $11.50.

Before we say goodbye to that old Australia, could we at least record some of its more memorable institutions?

- The old-style municipal pool. No water slide; no plunge pool; no sun protection; no cappuccino machine at the kiosk. In fact, no kiosk. Just a pool with a bull-necked manager who was a complete bastard. Fabulous!
- The tiny fibro beach house with lino on the floors and a Laminex kitchen table that seated eight. It was owned by a friend of Terry's aunt. It was shabby, noisy and stripped away stress like a high-suction hose.

- The pub with beer and nothing else. Ask for a red wine and the barman would give you a good long stare. He'd reluctantly agree to search out a bottle of shiraz, which he'd finally locate in the fridge. There was a steel trough in which to drop your cigarette butts and a dartboard up the end, the pattern of hits – mostly on the wall – testimony to decades of total inebriation.
- The really rough pub at the wrong end of a big town in Queensland. Most of the clientele wore sunglasses, with caps pulled down hard. When *Australia's Most Wanted* came on the TV, the whole front bar would empty.
- The country cafe whose owners invested in a cappuccino machine but were then unwilling to order the coffee beans to go with it. Arise the cheapuccino – steamed milk poured on a spoonful of International Roast, with a big serve of sugar, whether you wanted it or not. Delicious!
- The motel that cost $40 a night. Fair enough, it wasn't that good. The pillows were so thin you had to sleep with your elbow under your head, while the carpet recorded the story of previous occupants and their mishaps with various liquids. Strange fact: the sign outside advertising the presence of a pool was sometimes larger than the pool itself.
- The beachside kiosk selling ice-blocks to the kids. The pavement was so hot you had to jump

from foot to foot as you ordered, while the inadequate freezer meant the ice-blocks had all slumped out of shape. The owner? Of course he was surly; wouldn't you be, stuck in a hot bunker while everyone else was swimming? The kiosk has now been converted into an oyster and semillon bar owned by a TV chef. Kids can still order an ice-block, of course, but now it's called 'lemon sorbet on a stick' and costs $13.50.

- Clothes shops with no choice. Short sleeves or long? Blue or khaki? A pair of pants to go with it? Short or long? Whole shopping trip: ten minutes. Brilliant!
- Cake shops with no choice. Vanilla slice or lamington? One of each, thanks.
- A barber who made every customer look like an axe murderer. Sure, he was a menace with a pair of scissors but his shop did boast the world's biggest collection of decade-old copies of the *Australasian Post*. And he never tried to make conversation by asking about your holiday plans.

So farewell to the old Australia and hooray to the new. Let us take fond memories of each when we are all finally interred in Stonequarry Cemetery up on Golspie Road, where the views are fine and the grass is forever green.

The Lost Meals

Many people, me included, have been trying out a new diet – the 5:2 diet, otherwise known as intermittent fasting. What follows are some gastronomic notes on all the meals I've missed.

Tuesday 2 April: A delicious sorrel soup is not served for lunch. Afterwards there is an absence of asparagus, presented on a plate entirely bare of lightly grilled salmon. Hollandaise sauce, creamy yet tart, is not lightly drizzled onto the fish. A bottle of Alsatian gewürztraminer, produced by the Hoer family in the southern Tyrolean mountains, goes unopened.

Thursday 4 April: A robust meat pie is refused. The non-attendant meat is lamb, slow-cooked in the Greek style at just 120 degrees for four hours. The word 'tender' does not do justice to the effect of this sort of cooking. A sheet of puff pastry is then eschewed, the edges unable to turn crisp and golden brown after about twenty minutes in a hot oven. An innovative salad, composed of mint, pecans and walnuts, is waved away. A crisp craft cider from Michigan, made in the traditional manner, remains in the fridge.

Tuesday 9 April: Today I have the urge to avoid something really special. I decide to decline some crabmeat, flown in this morning from the clear waters of Western Australia, picked from the shell and ready for use. I avoid mixing this with a mêlée of spring onion, coriander leaves – freshly chopped is best! – sour cream, Tabasco and breadcrumbs. A high-quality olive oil is left unheated, its aroma failing to catch the nose and cause a momentary swoon. There's a perfect wine for this meal: West Australian semillon-sauvignon blanc, sourced from Margaret River and chilled to about 7 degrees Celsius. On no account should it be served.

Thursday 11 April: What's great about this diet is the feeling of choice. The only rule is that you eat nothing at all for twelve hours at a stretch – but it's entirely up to you which meals you forego. An amusing French choux pastry filled with crème pâtissière; a hefty serve of Bavarian pork knuckle, nestled beside some golden potato rosti; some prawns cooked in the zesty spices of Thailand – all can be refused with the sort of causal shrug that demonstrates a strong person with a real commitment to dieting. Today, for example, I decide to shun something very simple but quite delicious. Inside my fridge sit the perfect ingredients: three organic eggs, some chives, a little milk, butter and a small packet of smoked salmon. Can you guess? Of course, it's an omelette, warm and fluffy. In my mind's ear, I hear the ingredients singing from inside the fridge. 'Cook us up!' they chant; 'Give us a chance to show how well we work together!' Slid directly onto a plate from the hot pan, the omelette would demand four triangles of hot buttered toast, served on a separate plate in order to maintain maximum crunch. It's hard to imagine a more delicious repast towards which one could mumble, 'No thanks.'

Tuesday 16 April: *Oh my God I'm hungry.* It may be that I need to have an affair. Just to distract me from the incredible pain I'm in. The trouble is I don't really want an affair. All the same, if I were to refuse someone, I'd want them to be smart and attractive. I'm thinking of someone with a PhD in ancient history who enjoys wearing short skirts with leather boots. She'd have a mane of russet-coloured hair, strands of which would fall across that imperious forehead, her eyes sympathetic as she congratulated me on the progress of the diet. 'I think you are doing so well,' she'd say. 'Your body looks fantastic,' she'd add, her eyes, like those of a hungry cat, lingering on my rapidly firming torso. She'd then become worried about my pale face and start offering me titbits from her backpack: a hunk of Brie she happened to have, just warm enough that it had softened perfectly, along with a baguette which I now realise was poking out of her backpack all along. 'You're something special,' I'd tell her, politely declining both the affair and all the cheese. She'd look disappointed as she mounted her bicycle and headed off, the breadstick bobbing up and down as she pedalled away.

Thursday 18 April: I may be losing my mind. The food I'm refusing is no longer even food. Just an hour ago I started to look longingly at the tax papers on my desk. 'Just a nibble,' I found myself thinking. I suck hard on the end of a pen and get a mouthful of ink. Actually, it's quite refreshing. I must reassert mental discipline and refuse some normal food. A Rick Stein Sri Lankan fish curry would be perfect, made with salmon steaks cooked with tamarind and turmeric, plus the richness of coconut milk – the whole melange not served with a mango and lime chutney and lacking steamed basmati rice.

As I contemplate the flavours, I realise this may be the best meal I've avoided all month.

Chapter 2

In which Jeeves comes
to the rescue and Naomi
Wolf is given a hand

An Advice-like Grip

The world's self-help gurus want me to change. According to them, everything I do is wrong. I'm an anxious, self-doubting person who spends much of his life living in the past or dreaming of the future. I drink too much and work too hard. I overthink everything. My 'self-talk' has a fair measure of self-contempt, marinated in self-loathing and self-doubt. I lie awake at night contemplating all the things that have gone wrong that day, then arise in the morning and consider all that might go wrong in the day to come. I lack 'positive thinking'. I regularly cry over spilt milk.

Whole sections of the bookstore are now dedicated to helping people just like me. Week-long seminars are held, priced at a mere $10,000 a head. Magazine advice columns offer me and my kind the tantalising hope of a better life.

My only problem: I'm happy the way I am. I think other members of my tribe are happy too; we just don't have the overweening self-belief required to sing our own praises. After all, many of history's great achievers were anxious, self-doubting overthinkers. Certainly, all the interesting people I know have minds that circle around holding endless arguments with themselves. Tell that to the breezy, smiley crew in charge of the world of self-help and all you'll get is a look of concern.

Maybe it's time for a little defiance. I'd like to start a club for people who are anxious about everything but their over-anxiousness; a club for those who think positively about negative thoughts; and for those who have self-regard for their lack of self-regard.

No longer will we endure the smug tone of the Self-Help Police. Seen from our side of the paddock, most of what they have to say is simplistic dreck. It's the worst good advice in the world.

Bad Advice 1: Live in the present

This piece of advice is so often cited it's itself become a good reason for not living in the present, since so much of the 'present' now consists of people lecturing you about how you should live in it. In truth, the recollected past and the anticipated future are incredibly nourishing places. The present nearly always involves a soup of distractions; it contains the thing that's important, tangled up with the unimportant. Recollecting the moment you stood in front of a favourite painting, for example, is often better than the moment itself. In recollection you can strip away everything that stood in the way: your sore feet, the couple talking loudly behind you, the queue for admission. Memory pares down the moment to its essence. The same is true of the birth of a child, a kiss, a bushwalk. As memory, the experience is at its most pure, intense and unencumbered.

After remembering these things in blissful reverie, you can then anticipate similar experiences in the future, the hoped-for happenings fizzing in your mind.

This is not to disregard the present. The present, after all, is highly useful in providing the materials for both recollection and anticipation – those glorious periods in which you can escape the tiresome but much celebrated dictatorship of the present.

Bad Advice 2: Think positive

Have these people never read Seneca? It took three goes to kill the Roman philosopher – he opened his own veins, which didn't work; then took poison, which didn't work; then threw himself bleeding into a warm bath, which finally did the trick. Seneca, though, took it all in his stride. He'd spent a lifetime training his mind to think negatively. Leaping from bed in the morning, he'd consider all the things that could go wrong, and then – as the day went on – be pleasantly surprised by how well things went.

Compare that to the 'think positive' crowd who must spend every day in a funk of outrage over their shocked realisation that the world is an imperfect place.

And, on that last terrible day of poisoning and bloodletting, at least Seneca would have died with the pleasant satisfaction of getting it right: 'I knew today was going to be crap.'

Bad Advice 3: Be healthy

Of course it's good to be healthy, but this advice is normally so thoroughly bundled up with shame it often does more harm than good. Yes, people enjoy happier and longer lives if they avoid obesity. They also enjoy happier and longer lives if they are not laid low by anxiety, depression and self-contempt. Is our central problem that we ask too little of ourselves or that we demand too much? We hate ourselves for our every imperfection and then over-consume in various ways to suppress the shame of that imperfection. Then we over-consume some more in order to blot out the additional shame of that previous over-consumption. And so it goes. There are two epidemics underway in the West – obesity and depression. How interesting that both started just as people began obsessing over their bodies.

Bad Advice 4: Drink less

Have you tasted the 2011 Best's Bin No. 1 Shiraz? Lush, isn't it? And yet you still say, quoting official guidelines: one and a quarter standard glasses, then put the bottle away? You don't feel you're setting the bar, in both meanings of the word, a little high?

Bad Advice 5: Don't focus on past errors

This is the modern version of 'don't cry over spilt milk'. There is still, however, the question of how the milk was spilt in the first place. Maybe you need a different bucket, without holes. Maybe you should carry the bottle in your hands rather than balancing it on your nose. Perhaps a motorised Lazy Susan isn't the best idea for a breakfast table. Crying over the spilt milk is how we focus the mind to solve whatever problem is causing the milk to spill. Consider, for instance, the little UHT packets you find in motels: people's unwillingness to cry over spilt milk may be the reason they've never been redesigned – despite decades in which they have spilt milk over all who've tried to open one.

Bad Advice 6: Smell the roses

This is a staple of the graduation speech. A person in their late fifties, having already achieved much in life, tells an audience of young people to slow down. Naturally, they never took this advice themselves; when they were young, they threw themselves at life. That's how they became sufficiently successful to deliver this speech which, frankly, is going on a bit. Don't they have a meeting to get to? A company to run? The truth is that good things happen when we burn the candle at both ends.

So here's to us – we who spend our lives in a daydreamed past and an anticipated future; we who drink too much, work too hard and plan for the worst. We hear the advice that is constantly proffered. We're just unsure we want to take it.

Count Me Out

How did you go when you last filled in your census form? Is your marriage still intact? Amazing if it is: the whole thing seemed designed to encourage divorce. Consider Question 48: 'How many hours did you spend on housework?' That query alone will cause World War III in most households.

For a start, there are the definitional issues. Is making home-brewed beer 'a necessity of life, just as important as doing the laundry'? Or 'a complete waste of money, plus your home-brew tastes like bum'? Ditto the half hour I spent alphabetising my Elvis CDs. Was it: 'a much-needed clean-up, making life easier for all residents of the household'? Or 'time wasting of the first order, especially since you should have filed them in order of his body weight at the time of recording'?

Perhaps you can spot the sweet tones of Jocasta in these comments. Jocasta has long alleged that I do only stunt housework, which she defines as 'housework involving a ladder'. 'Sure,' she says, 'if there's a lightbulb to change, you're the man. You love it: it involves maximum attention, maximum fuss and it only needs doing once a year.'

In return I point out my sterling work in the ironing department, even including the ruched collars and complicated skirts that have ended up in the Too Hard Basket. She says none of it counts since I enjoy doing the ironing; a principle she doesn't apply to herself, rapidly including in her own tally the hours she spends sitting watching *Inspector Rex* with our dog in her continuing bid to teach him German.

She calculates her own housework at fifteen hours a week, and reluctantly accepts my self-tally of sixteen hours a week, a calculation she describes as 'speculative fiction of the highest order'.

Other questions prove equally tricky. Who is Person One? Should it be judged on income level, age or whichever of you first spotted the house in the real estate window? 'I think it's me,' Jocasta says, 'on account that I have more to put up with. Person One is the person who has most to endure.' She takes her time with the word 'endure' so it hangs in the air like a bitter black cloud within which is contained every pair of male socks fished from under the couch, every towel left on the bedroom floor, and every argument over whose turn it is to scrub out the shower recess.

We move onwards through the form. Jocasta reluctantly allows me to describe myself as 'male', but only after a lengthy discussion of my belly, which she describes as 'definitely third trimester'.

We move on to Question 5: 'What is the person's relationship to Person Two?'

'What am I meant to put here?' Jocasta asks. 'There seems to be no spot for "indentured slave".'

She flashes me a sassy little smile and we move on to Question 8: 'Where does the person usually live?' – which causes Jocasta to pause once more. 'Do they mean in my mind or in reality?' she asks. 'Because in my mind I'm living in a Spanish fishing village with a strong but gentle *hombre* called Pedro, who sees to all my personal needs.'

'Do you know the postcode of Pedro's place?' I ask absentmindedly but Jocasta just shakes her head. 'He lives on a fishing boat in the harbour.'

At this point Jocasta seems lost in a reverie and so I sit and let my mind wander. Whenever I take a shower, some of the water splashes onto the shower door. Surely this counts as cleaning. It could be that I've understated my tally.

Jocasta focuses back on the form and tackles Question 16 about 'languages other than English'. 'I'll put down Neanderthal for both children,' she says, 'as they largely communicate in a series of inaudible grunts. The census people want to know if they can speak English, but as their mother how can I be sure? I'll be able to tell once they turn thirty; perhaps they could get back to me then?'

I read out Question 21 – 'Does Person One need help being understood?' – and Jocasta responds with enthusiasm. 'Yes,' she says, 'I find it almost impossible to make myself understood. For instance, the phrase: "Could someone else occasionally clean the shower recess?" Is there a particular part of that phrase which is leaving people around here baffled? Could I employ simpler words in order to get my meaning across? Perhaps you'd all rather I got the dog to bark the message in German, *Inspector Rex*-style: *Könnte jemand anderes zu reinigen die Dusche Vertiefung?*'

I yawn, stretch and get up off the couch, leaving Jocasta to finish the form. A couple of glasses of home-brew might warm the somewhat frosty atmosphere.

'Glass of bum?' I ask cheerily as I stand in front of the fridge.

'Yeah, sure,' Jocasta says. 'A glass of bum would be very nice.'

As I pour the beer, a question suggests itself. The census is meant to count the number of intact households in Australia. But do they mean intact at the start of census week or intact by the end?

Sebastian Faulks and the
Impending Doom

'Best-selling writer Sebastian Faulks is to breathe new life into much-loved characters Jeeves and Wooster after being approached by the estate of P.G. Wodehouse.'
– The Independent (UK)

I was at my desk wishing I'd never said 'yes' to this novel-writing caper. I don't know about you, but the phrase 'chapter one' always seems to come nimbly to mind, speeding out of the blocks and plonking itself onto the page, then things rather go to pieces.

One stares at the wall, then at the floor, then at the wall again, all in the hope that, in the absence of your eye, some fellow has daubed the paintwork with a workable plot. Alas, they have not and so with a cry of 'Come on, Faulks, show your mettle', one is finally forced to begin typing.

I decided to begin with Bertie Wooster, describing

him *striding into his club, the Drones, wearing a pair of tartan pants, a striped shirt and an immaculately tailored white jacket, purchased on a recent trip to Monaco.*

I leant back and contemplated the phrase with some pleasure. I was off and running. It was then I heard a delicate clearing of the throat. Ah, Jeeves. That man's ability to glide noiselessly into a room was remarkable. He'd positioned himself so he had a full view of the computer screen.

'What is it Jeeves? Can't you see I'm doing battle here, wrestling with the English language?'

'I'm sure you will prove its equal, sir,' said Jeeves in that smooth way of his.

'Yes, well, carry on.'

I turned to face the keyboard only to be distracted by another festival of throat clearing.

'What's wrong, Jeeves? You're not going on the sick list?'

'If I may speak frankly, sir, the mode of dress you describe is quite out of keeping for the character of Mr Wooster. There are other characters in Mr Wodehouse's *oeuvre* who might avail themselves of such a jacket – Lord Worplesdon comes to mind – but never, if I might be so bold, a member of the Drones.'

It's at moments like these when one must make a stance. True, Jeeves is the world's most famous man-servant, but I, dash it, am Sebastian Faulks, author of fourteen books, with a CBE for services to literature.

'Jeeves, I'm grateful for your counsel but a skilful writer often brings a flash of the unexpected to the clothing of his characters. In one of my own novels, I featured a pair of Churchill lace-ups that were virtually a character note in leather. Dash it, a chap has the right to select a jacket without landing himself in the pea and ham.'

'Very well, sir.'

Jeeves has the ability to express agreement in a way that suggests one has just been set adrift on an iceberg, with a fractious polar bear as one's sidekick.

I've long considered myself a man of iron, but even men of iron know there are moments when one must bend. As Jeeves watched over my shoulder, I idly tapped the backwards delete button, removing in turn Bertie's jacket, his shirt and then his pants, until the world's greatest comic creation was standing there, naked except for a pair of white y-fronts. It half-reminded me of a quote: 'I had poured him out of his clothes and had forgotten to say when.'

'If I may, sir?'

Jeeves took my seat in front of the computer and, with a few calm keystrokes, assisted the Wooster into a pair of grey trousers, a pale blue shirt and dark jacket. 'A Drones club tie might be added, if sir permits, tied firmly in order to achieve a butterfly effect.'

Once Jeeves had engaged the grey matter, the motor fairly purred. The man must eat nothing but goji berries.

'Jeeves?' I inquired.

'Yes, sir.'

'I might pop out for a quick restorative. Lubricate the old adjectives and all that.'

'Very wise, sir.'

'And it would be a shame to see the computer sitting idle in my absence. Deadline looming and all that rot.'

'It would indeed be an adverse outcome if the machine were not engaged in the production of successive sentences leading to a satisfactory narrative.'

We Faulkses are sometimes a little weak in the head, but I took a stab at his meaning.

'So, if I were to whip out and belt down a couple of liver-ticklers ...'

'While you are absent, I would endeavour to utilise the machine to achieve the completion of an artefact acceptable to the publisher.'

'Jeeves, you are a good egg.'

'Oh, and sir? I wouldn't leave via the sitting room. A representative of the publishing house is waiting there to receive the completed manuscript.'

'Really? I thought the deadline ...'

'It passed yesterday, sir. I took the liberty of giving the gentleman some preliminary chapters which I prepared earlier. He is reading them currently and has expressed his satisfaction as to the contents. If you were to shimmy down the drainpipe on the outside of the building, he'll be gone, with the complete manuscript in hand, by the time you return from the club.'

'Well done, Jeeves.'

'I endeavour to give satisfaction, sir.'

I smiled at the thought of the liquid life-givers that were about to come my way.

'I'll leave it to you, Jeeves. Now where is this drainpipe of which you speak so highly?'

Bolt from the Blue

A young female friend tells me it's hard to get to know the boys at high school parties because 'they just talk about themselves'. Naturally, I was shocked: the old men of the tribe have failed to pass on the ancient secrets of meeting the opposite sex.

Rule one is always ask about her. This goes back many millennia to when the first caveman stumbled on the first cavewoman and sympathetically inquired about her efforts to achieve a work–life balance. She had a wildebeest that needed gutting, he had the evening free, and that's how the human race began.

It's been the same ever since. Properly informed teenage boys, in service of their biological destiny, have politely inquired about matters in which they have no possible interest, including, in extreme cases:

- *Lovely dress! Is it from Zara?*
- *I love Justin Bieber, too! When did you first discover him?*
- *Tell me more about veganism. It sounds like it could be right for me.*

I admit it's tough to find something to talk about. When I was sixteen, a friend used to take a medium-sized bolt to teenage parties. When he found himself in front of a girl, he'd be red-faced and tongue-tied but, in an effort of self-mastery, would pull the bolt from his pocket and display it on an outstretched yet shaking hand. She'd say, 'What's that?' He'd say, 'It's a bolt,' and the conversation would be off and running.

Crucially, though, he'd then turn the conversation back to the girl, as in the inquiry: 'So do you have a collection of bolts, too?'

This sort of smooth, debonair style is clearly missing in the current generation of young men. Luckily, I'm in a position to help.

What's crucial is to express interest in whatever is being said, however much of a stretch. For example:

- *It's just so great to meet someone as concerned as I am about tropical deforestation.*
- *I agree with you about the engine capacity of the Lamborghini Gallardo Spyder but do you think the output is delivered more smoothly in the Porsche Carrera GT?*
- *So who is your very favourite Kardashian?*

Of course, it used to be easier for young people to meet. When I was growing up, we'd spend long evenings gathered around the piano, wishing one of us could play. Into the deathly silence, we'd always try to stammer out a question: 'I just adore Germaine Greer. My only criticism: she's not tough enough on the men. What's your view?'

More importantly, we'd try to turn ourselves into the sort of young chaps who'd interest these particular young women. Preparation was everything, with your teenage bedroom kitted out to give the false impression you were a sensitive intellectual. Copies of *Soldier of Fortune* were hidden away and replaced by a purposefully well-thumbed edition of *The Collected Poems of Emily Dickinson*. Neil Diamond's *Hot August Night* was banished from its usual place on the turntable and replaced with an ECM jazz record from a Norwegian minimalist called, as I remember it, Terje Rypdal.

And Greer's *The Female Eunuch*, the world's least likely erotic aid, was placed on the bedside table.

This was the late '70s and many of us shared the optimistic belief that we were intellectuals. Thus most girls of my acquaintance demanded a familiarity with the latest edition of the *Guardian Weekly*. Indeed, from the ages of sixteen to twenty-one, nearly all my romantic assignations occurred with the direct involvement of the *Guardian Weekly*, so much so that I still get a small erotic charge from the mere mention of that robust and impressive masthead.

Whatever the preparation, it's important to make the most of any social gathering. On this score, don't be too nervous. As a young man, it's important to realise that, just as you have come to a party to meet girls, so the girls have come with the intention of meeting boys: just ones who are older, smarter and better looking than you.

This is not the point to give up. This is the point at which you engage the opposite sex in conversation, each question perfectly tailored to suit your companion:

- *Baby dolphins? Really? What a surprise, because I love them, too.*
- *What did you think of the Booker shortlist?*
- *Thank God they've finally put vodka and orange in a goon sack.*

Ask her name. Ask about her hobbies. Ask about her job. And then express interest:

- *Claudine ... wow, are you French?*
- *Tenpin bowling? Daggy? No way!*
- *So, let me get this straight: your part-time job is to remove the guts from the chicken and then spray out the carcass with water? How fascinating. I've always been interested in poultry production methods. Perhaps you could tell me more over a drink?*

Remember, the future of the human race depends on you. In the past century alone, at least seven billion similar conversations must have occurred. Surely, for the sake of humanity, you can manage one more.

If not, try going with a bolt in your pocket.

Frog to Princess: Kiss Harder

Could I have a bit of sympathy, please? It's true I don't have halitosis, varicose veins or fallen arches, but I do have warts. Yes, warts. Two hideous deformities on the knuckles of my left hand, just where they are most noticeable. I'm convinced it's the evil within coming out. The unattractive, hunched, gnome-like figure that lurks inside me is trying to push through. Cleverly, I've resisted and this is as far as he's got – these strange, medieval-looking protuberances.

Here's the thing: the doctors can do nothing. My GP, with only a slight smile, suggested I go and dance naked in the graveyard at midnight. That, she said, was as likely to achieve a good outcome as anything she could recommend.

At the local medical centre, the staff were keener to accumulate billing hours, so they had me visit every two weeks so the damn things could be attacked with liquid nitrogen. The doctors involved varied in style – from the kindly yet cautious lady doctor who sprayed the thing for about a second, to a gruff, older chap, apparently from the US Navy SEAL school of medicine, who said, 'Let's blast the bastards good … they won't be coming back when I am finished.'

Outcome of both procedures: identical. The warts grow back.

I then decided to mount my own jihad against the warts, painting them with some gunk obtained from the chemist.

After a week, the stuff had burnt away half my hand, while having no impact on the warts.

Next I tried home-applied nitrogen, squirting away with a canister purchased from the supermarket. This left the warts momentarily dazed, but they soon sloughed off their gloom and began looking for their next challenge.

Around this time, I appeared on a morning TV show and the discussion turned to wedding rings. I gestured to my right hand to show that I didn't wear one myself, but the host corrected me, saying 'The wedding ring goes on the left hand'. She reached over, took my left hand and held it to the camera, demonstrating the correct placement of a wedding ring. Short of fighting her for possession of my arm, I was powerless to resist.

I could see the cameramen come in for a close up, then reel back in horror. What began as an amusing chat about etiquette had turned into a segment from *World's Grossest Medical Horrors*.

How come we can put a man on the moon but are powerless over warts?

Lots of people seem to have had a warty period. One friend, a farming type, shrugs and says he just slices them off with a penknife. Others talk about going to top Macquarie Street specialists, who, upon payment of many thousands of dollars, surgically remove each of the invaders.

Outcome of both procedures: identical. The warts grow back.

They are also shrouded in mystery, subject of the strangest beliefs. 'You should get someone to buy your warts. If they give you twenty cents, the wart will go away.' The person who told me this, by the way, is a nurse of twenty years' experience. She confided that she lacked the twenty cents to test the theory by buying mine, presumably due to the poor pay rates in the health system. Another friend offered me a 'subliminal sleep programming' CD, in which the words 'warts away' are chanted throughout the night. This may well work but I can't see it being good for my relationship. Speaking of which, Jocasta thinks the warts are hilarious. She points them out to everyone just so she can have the chance to say, 'I still love him, warts and all.'

When walking together, I force myself to trot along with her to my right. It's more common, of course, for the man to walk with the woman to his left: that way we can pull our sword from its scabbard and swing outwards should any dragons happen along. Now, as a warty man, dragon safety can no longer be my first priority. Standing on my right, Jocasta can at least reach for my hand and not get the warty one.

George Orwell famously wrote: 'At age fifty, every man has the face he deserves.' Fair enough – but what did I do to deserve this left hand? Warts, after all, don't get a good rap in the culture. Warts are what distinguishes the wicked witch from the good one. In *Harry Potter*, the school is called Hogwarts so as to summon up the supernatural. Frogs are always covered in warts, which disappear once the frog turns into the prince.

When might this happen for me? Jocasta gives her warty frog a peck on the cheek, declaring that this may well awaken the prince within.

It doesn't work.

'Kiss harder, Princess,' I say, presenting my puckered lips. And indeed she gives it a thorough go.

With the right sales pitch, I could work this to my advantage.

At this point, having admitted my problem in print and on the radio, kindly people began writing to me about their preferred wart-removal method. To be precise: 137 letters and emails. As a result I find myself able to present at least thirty different cures and – by statistical analysis – list the Top Three Folk Remedies. And, since I still have the warts, I can test out the most popular cures. Don't say I don't put my body on the line.

First, to the multiplicity of cures. Karen recommends the sap from a poinsettia bush. Trevor, Kathryn, two Davids and a Rowley recommend the milk from a thistle. Bill recommends breathing on them and Georgie says to take two kelp tablets a day for three weeks.

Caro then invites me to urinate on my hand first thing in the morning. I rapidly decide against testing this method, however many votes it receives.

Sandie and others recommend vitamin E oil. Mick suggests taping a piece of onion over my warts for a few days. Jenny cites the same technique but using oranges and, in her cure, the fruit is eaten.

As I open the letters and emails, things are getting weirder. Anne, Alicia and Keith all recommend fetching a snail from the garden and rubbing the mucus over the warts each day. Mary instructs me to spit on them first thing in the morning, then offers the helpful addendum: 'PS: You cannot use another person's spit.'

Minnie recommends cod liver oil, applied topically. Helen says that's no good; it's got to be salmon oil, taken orally. Paul says to attack the things with tweezers, 'but don't be a girl and cry'. Get stuck in, he says.

Sue, Judy and seven others suggest covering them with clear nail polish.

Barbara says she had a wool-classer boyfriend in the 1950s and he, along with the shearers, never suffered from warts because of the lanolin in the wool. I should give that a go, she says – the lanolin, not the shearer boyfriend.

Lynne says hers disappeared sometime during a sixteen-hour labour, giving birth to her first son, and suggests I close my eyes and fantasise I'm giving birth.

You think that's weird? We have barely started on the weird.

Alan, at age nine, was taken by his mother to see an old Irish lady. She cut an apple into quarters and rubbed each of them over the warts. Alan was then told to bury the quarters in the four corners of her backyard. Result: his warts were gone in a week.

Geoff says his teacher at Kingsgrove De La Salle, Brother Clement, a good guy, would take a child's hand and rub at the wart with his heavily nicotine-stained fingers. The wart would shrivel to nothing. There was quite a queue for the service.

In the 1950s, Frank lived in a small country town in which the cure was to ask a local called 'Old George Kearns' to stare at your warts, at which point they would fall off. If Old George wasn't around, you'd tell his son, who'd ask his father to think about your warts when he arrived home. As soon as he got around to it, the warts would disappear.

And Anne says she'd get an empty washbasin, take it into the backyard at night and wash her hands in moonlight.

What was the cure most often recommended? Banana peel, white side pressed against the wart and then fixed in place with sticking plaster, as recommended by twelve people. The banana peel method is hence my first experiment; this despite the fact that a cyclone had just wiped out the Queensland banana crop and they were priced at $15 a kilo. My correspondents must think I'm made of money.

Each day I strap two bits of peel to my hands. They have an amazing effect, rapidly eating away the warts, somewhat assisted by a bit of action with a pumice stone. Nine days into my experiment, the warts are almost gone. I had intended to test the nail polish cure and the milk thistle cure but I won't have a chance.

What to do about the rough patch left behind? Thoroughly converted to the world of folk cures, I grab an empty washbasin and head out into the darkened backyard.

It's nothing washing my hands in moonlight won't fix. Plus a bit more puckering-up in close proximity to Jocasta.

A Sinking Sensation

The moment of clarity came half a second before the liquid hit. I was kneeling on the kitchen floor, sucking on a length of plastic pipe, the other end snaking up over the sink and then into the drain. If I sucked hard, a vacuum would pull the water out of the blocked drain and into my bucket. Then I could pour drain cleaner into the sink, leaving it to settle directly on the blockage where it could do its caustic good works. What could go wrong?

At first, it all goes well: the water gushes into the bucket, the drain cleaner fizzes in a satisfying way. Then I turn on the taps so the water can gurgle through the unblocked drain. Except it doesn't. If the blockage doesn't clear, the pack says, repeat steps one to five. I'm good at following orders; very obedient chap, me. Okay. 'Step one, clear any water that's on top of the blockage.'

Back goes the hose, snaking down into the drain. Again I position myself on the ground near my bucket, taking an almighty suck at the end of the tube. Perhaps, at this point, you are ahead of me. First time around, the water was certainly unpleasant – dirty sink water, somewhat greasy. Second time around, the water is cleaner. Except it now contains enough drain cleaner to kill an elephant: this being the water that is currently travelling towards my mouth.

There's an excellent poem by Edward Lear, or it could have been Ogden Nash or, at a pinch, Spike Milligan, which features a man electrocuting himself because he couldn't bring himself to ring a tradesman. I can't summon up the words from childhood, not while the toxic waste is hurtling down the tube, although I'm sure it featured a chap teetering atop a chair as the electric current headed his way. It strikes me that I am in exactly the same predicament, the drain cleaner serving in the role of the electric current. I have often imagined myself into literature, normally playing the role of Atticus Finch or Odysseus or, at the very least, James Bond. Yet here I am re-enacting a comic poem about a suicidal moron. Instead of trying to remember who wrote it, perhaps I should focus on removing my mouth from the end of the hose. Still, it's hard to concentrate, as the author of the poem – much like the fast-approaching drain cleaner – is right on the tip of my tongue.

It's true I am burdened with overconfidence when it comes to home repairs. I'm the one who decided to replace a faulty bearer under our bathroom floor, declaring that a carpenter was unnecessary for such basic maintenance. The result was a talking toilet that appeared to moan when anyone walked towards it. Guests to our home would observe that, while the post of 'toilet' was perhaps not the most glorious position to occupy in a household, they had never heard one remonstrate so vigorously about fulfilling its duties.

The talking toilet has, over time, settled down. It now just sighs loudly if someone heavy approaches. This is understandable in a way, although somewhat uncaring of the feelings of the overweight.

There is also a handmade bookshelf, bolted to the wall above my desk, the strength of whose bolts I question every time I return a heavy book. What a perfect end to my life if, after consulting the *Collins Thesaurus* for the appropriate word, the shelf, its burden increased by the replacement of that single volume, heaved itself forwards and downwards, leaving me dead, deceased, defunct, departed, extinct and gone.

Certainly, it would be a better end than that provided by the drain cleaner, which seems to cackle with laughter as it hurtles towards union with my mouth. Right now, I'm not in a position to reach for the thesaurus, sitting as I am on the kitchen floor, but it seems clear the drain cleaner will soon render my mouth wounded, scalded, injured, ill-treated, abused and hurt.

I sense a figure behind me: it's Jocasta. She's been hovering in the kitchen ever since I employed what she calls 'that ominous phrase': 'I can fix it.'

'There's drain cleaner in that water,' she says, puzzlement crossing her features. 'Why are you sucking it?'

I need to explain that I'm not as dumb as I look, and that I have long ago – as much as a tenth of a second ago – realised my peril but then my mind had become preoccupied with the poem, which was either written by Ogden Nash or Edward Lear or, at an outside chance, Spike Milligan. Jocasta will probably know. I remove the tube and look up, ready to ask my question. As it happens, I'm pretty much in time; just a splash of drain cleaner hits my top lip, leaving a slight burning sensation.

'You don't happen to know the name of the poet who wrote about the Lord who electrocuted ...' I ask, but Jocasta is shaking her head and peering beneath the sink.

'First up,' she says, 'the poet you were thinking of is Hilaire Belloc and the poem is called "Lord Finchley".

'*Lord Finchley*,' she recites,

'*tried to mend the Electric Light*
Himself. It struck him dead: And serve him right!
It is the business of the wealthy man
To give employment to the artisan.'

From my vantage point on the floor, I give her a round of applause.

She acknowledges my praise before fixing me with a quizzical look. 'That aside, why didn't you just remove the S-bend.'

I have a perfectly good answer for that but my lip feels a bit burny. Better, I think, not to put it under any additional pressure.

A Bum Biography

Naomi Wolf has written a whole book about her sacred space, with the title *Vagina: A new biography*. She argues the vagina is the most important part of the body, the seat of all wisdom and the key to a woman's sense of self. As she puts it at one point: '... the vagina is a gateway to women's happiness and to her creative life.'

This is all very well but what about the rest of our bodies? It only seems fair that other body parts are given the same intense, somewhat poetic, attention.

Index Finger: A new biography
The vagina might be a really terrific body part, you'll have no argument from me on that score, but so is the index finger. Oh, mighty body part that can turn from admonishing a fellow road user to beckoning a prospective lover, and yet still be pressed into service when the need comes to scratch an itch. Everyone praises Steve Jobs for developing the iPhone and the tablet computer, but where would he have been without the index finger? There would just be a whole lot of

people on the bus mashing vainly at their smartphones with their elbows.

Leg: A new biography
The leg is the loneliest body part, particularly the male leg, asked to work away in the dark, rarely allowed to see its identical twin toiling away next door. From an early age legs are covered by trousers – a sort of bottom-half burqa – and spoken about only when they fail. 'Oh, you're limping' or 'Here's old Hopalong'. No mention, you'll notice, of the large and growing stomach that the legs are required to carry around; no acknowledgment the uneven gait might be caused by an increasing load being silently borne. Oh no, it's all down to the poor old legs. It's like a Third World country down there: forced to do all the donkey work yet afforded so few of life's pleasures. All the legs want is the occasional compliment: 'Oh, I notice you're not limping. Your legs must be doing an awfully good job.'

Bum: A new biography
Naomi may well believe in the supremacy of what is sometimes termed 'the front bottom', but where would she be without a real bottom? As the writer Tim Winton established in his influential volume *The Bugalugs Bum Thief*, human beings missing their bums are not able to sit down. They lower themselves onto a chair and simply slip off. Yes, a vagina is a real boon but only if you have enough energy to make the most of it, having not been on your feet all day.

Elbow: A new biography

You can imagine a world without elbows: it's basically the zombie apocalypse. Offices would have to be bigger, to accommodate people typing with their arms outstretched. And, to drive a car, you'd have to be seated a full metre away from the wheel. Frankly, it's a bleak place all round. A world without elbows is a world without soup: the stuff becomes impossible to consume. Solid foods, meanwhile, would have to be eaten directly off the plate, using the same method as cows in the field. Or it could be suspended on thin ropes from the ceiling, whereupon guests could stretch their necks like so many hungry giraffes, nibbling on some low-hanging lamb chops. Alcohol would be more problematic: serving it in dog bowls might be the best idea, with guests on hands and knees slurping the last of your Koonunga Hill shiraz.

Mouth: A new biography

Talk about multitasking: breathing, eating and speaking – all achieved through the same slot worked into the front of the face. The lips can be opened, the sides curling upwards, to create a friendly smile when you walk into a shop. The same device is then used to issue a polite instruction to the person running the shop: 'I'll have a pie with sauce, thanks mate,' the tongue leaping around the mouth like a Russian gymnast. Then there's a two-minute wait – during which the mouth is being used to inhale and exhale air – after which the microwave finishes its work and the pie is handed over. At this point the same slot is used to both thank the man ('Thanks mate') and eat the pie. *Then* – oh, what immortal hand or eye could frame thy fearful symmetry? – the lips narrow to create an airtight vacuum around a straw, the better to drink the milkshake you have subsequently purchased to wash down the pie. The sigh of satisfaction at the end again employs the same device, installed conveniently in the front of the face, just where you'd want it to be, so the eyes might better assess the food being ingested, while the nose double-checks it's not off.

After all that, you'd be mad not to offer the world a smile – a smile that expresses your satisfaction at the joyful service provided by your mouth, bum, index fingers, elbows and legs.

The vagina? Don't get me wrong: absolutely marvellous. It's the whole machine, though, that's really something special.

Chapter 3

In which J.D. Salinger helps explain the virtues of the everyday, George Clooney provides some grooming tips and Tiffany is encouraged to stop screaming

The Clooney

When is a man too old for floppy hair? Jocasta has the answer and it's right now. 'You're too old for it,' she says. 'You need to get a Clooney.' She indicates the television screen on which an interview with George Clooney is in progress. George is by turn witty, self-deprecating, sensitive and politically right on. He also talks of his ownership of a mansion on the shore of Italy's Lake Como and the excellent wine cellar he has amassed there. The head of the United Nations came the other night for dinner, he reveals, yet somehow this doesn't sound like bragging. His grey hair is clipped in a way that makes him look both virile and intelligent.

'Yes,' Jocasta says dreamily. 'You need a Clooney.'

It's unclear whether she means just the haircut. She may mean a Clooney house, a Clooney wine cellar or a Clooney line in self-deprecating banter. Maybe she'd prefer me to be an international film star with writing and directing credits and a role as an international peace envoy, all of which might be difficult to achieve from my current starting point.

A week later she returns to the subject. 'The floppy hair has to go. It would be fine for a man in his twenties. George is your age and *he* has a Clooney. Besides which, your hair reminds me of your father.'

Over the years I've been forced to modify much of my behaviour because Jocasta says 'it reminds me of your father'. Stripy shirts, hound's-tooth jackets and drinking heavily before breakfast – all have had to go. But the hair? Whatever his other faults, my father had a magnificent head of hair. As he strolled down to his favourite Bondi bar in the late afternoon, it was like watching a peacock in courtship mode, his Brylcreem glinting in the sunlight.

Still, maybe Jocasta is right. My current hairstyle was adopted at age nineteen. I walked into a place in suburban Brisbane and asked for a 'Christopher-Isherwood-Cambridge-in-the-1920s-thanks', and when the hairdresser looked puzzled, added, 'You know, floppy, like Bryan Ferry.'

The style created that day looked good for at least three decades. Yet I now look in the mirror, the young hair flopped over the ageing, lined forehead, the skin a little pasty, the eyes rheumy. It's the look summed up by the phrase 'faded roué'.

More to the point, why shouldn't I bend to Jocasta's will? I've asked Jocasta to change aspects of herself over the years. I use the phrase 'it reminds me of your mother', but delivered at such low volume there is credible deniability, as in: 'I said what? No way. I just have a cough.' If I perform this act with sufficient doe-eyed sincerity, Jocasta becomes convinced that she's hearing some voice of wisdom from within and acts accordingly. Within a week, she's abandoned her mother's hairstyle, arguing techniques or infamous recipe for apricot chicken.

I'm sitting out the back with a glass of red when Jocasta approaches me with a firm plan.

'I think you need to go and see Shane,' she says, using the sombre tone with which one recommends a visit to a chaplain, funeral director or tax accountant. Shane's our hairdresser and I make an appointment for the weekend. On the morning of the visit, an email pops up from Jocasta, who is using the computer in the other room. It has nothing but an internet link. I click on the address. It's a website containing several pictures of George Clooney with a Clooney.

Dutifully I print out the best one, take it with me and present it to Shane.

'I want this,' I say.

He says, 'I know.' Jocasta has already spoken to him about it.

Shane gets to work, the photo of Clooney propped up against the mirror. I can sense other clients pointing and laughing as they walk past this hairdressing diorama. It should have a label: 'The Optimistic in Search of the Miraculous'.

Shane's scissors clip away. 'More of a shearer than a stylist,' he observes as vast quantities of hair fall to the ground. Whole squads of apprentices will be required to remove the detritus. This new diorama needs a new title: 'Here Lieth One Man's Youth'.

Yet slowly, as Shane clips, something miraculous happens. From the ruins of my face something new emerges. Younger? Certainly. Less try-hard? Oh, yes. More intelligent? Oh, at least 15 IQ points has been added.

I stare into the mirror as Shane finally puts down his scissors.

'I look like George Clooney.'

'Well, you only had to ask.'

A customer wandering past looks at my image in the mirror and then at the photo: 'You've made him look like George Clooney.'

Shane again: 'It's all part of the service.'

I arrive home and Jocasta is waiting for me. She swoons as I walk up the corridor, grabbing onto a bookshelf for support.

'It's amazing,' she says. 'I hardly recognise you.'

I gather her in an embrace and lean forward for the kiss.

'Oh, George,' she says, 'it's been so long.'

I make a mental note to go in for a clip more often.

The Trapdoor

The Space Cadet has been watching the BBC's new version of Sherlock Holmes. He seems to have the episodes on a loop, endlessly watching them back to back. He has always loved things he can watch or hear; he has never been so keen on sitting down to read. I don't know why. The house is full of books. From when he was born, we read to him. We have told him about the joy of books; the thrill of having a story at hand, this trapdoor into another world that can be slipped into your coat pocket.

When we say this, he rolls his eyes. He shrugs his shoulders. He says, 'I'll wait for the film, thanks.' This causes us great sadness. We feel we have failed him. Where did we go wrong?

I leave the room. I walk the dog. When I return there is silence from the room with the TV. I walk in and find him sitting on the couch. He is intently studying the screen of his mobile phone.

'I've just downloaded a couple of Arthur Conan Doyle short stories,' he says. 'They're very good, you know. Great storyteller!'

He says this in a tone of reproach, as if to say, 'Why didn't you ever tell me about this reading thing? I really recommend it, it's quite engrossing.'

I'm struck by an urge to throttle him. His first book could be his last. I could march towards the couch, wrapping my hands around his throat, shouting, 'This is what I've been trying to tell you for most of your life.'

Luckily, I'm on my way out the door, heading to a literary festival. I leave my son and his one book, and tumble into a whole world of books.

Australian novelist Kate Forsyth is one of the speakers. She explains how she became captivated by fiction after being attacked by a dog when she was two years old. The dog nearly killed her; over the next seven years she spent more time in hospital than out. The dog's fangs penetrated her skull. Among many other injuries, her left tear duct was destroyed; when she cried, her tears would poison her body. Books, she says, became her solace.

I was attacked by a dog at a similar age. My injuries were not so bad, although I was able to locate the teeth marks in my skull until my early teenage years. As I listen to Kate, a thought occurs: maybe a vicious dog attack is required to create an enthusiastic reader. I look around at this room full of readers. They don't appear to bear any visible teeth marks, yet who knows what other problems they have suffered.

I've read the autobiographies of many bookish types. Jeanette Winterson, in *Why Be Happy When You Could Be Normal?*, describes how she became a reader. There was no dog involved. Just an insane Pentecostal mother who thought Jeanette was the devil sent by God to torment her. Then there is Caitlin Moran, who describes how she was turned into a reader by intense loneliness, poverty and social isolation. Again, no dog. But plenty of problems.

Another writer at the festival, Kirsten Tranter, talks of being 'a bookish, lonely child', and this chimes with me. I certainly had an odd upbringing. I grew up in a normal-looking family but never felt like the favourite, which is hard when you are an only child.

Then my mother left, my father took to drink, and I started wheezing.

When I think about my favourite authors and their childhoods, the stories begin to merge in my mind – a sea of bedridden asthmatics, dog-attack victims and abandoned children. Readers often report this sense of being on the outer when they were growing up: 'I didn't fit in and so took refuge in this other world.' In retrospect, we probably fitted in better than we thought. As I've written in one of my own books, it now strikes me as remarkable that the 'cool' kids, perhaps five per cent of the schoolyard, managed to convince the other ninety-five per cent that we were the odd ones out. The cool kids may have had the greatest social confidence but their maths was terrible. And so was ours for believing them.

Yet, even if our sense of oddness was a little overplayed, books were still a ticket to other worlds. I remember being twelve years old, sitting on my own on the edge of the school oval, reading a book I just loved: *Right Ho, Jeeves* by P. G. Wodehouse. (Okay, I know, a picture does form.)

A swaggering oaf approached and trod on my book, just for the fun of it. I was a cowardly child but still leapt up to confront him. Alas, my choice of language may have been influenced by my reading material. 'You can't do that, you cad,' I said. 'You're a complete bounder!'

I gave him a little shove. And then he laughed and punched me in the nose. It may have been the first time the word 'bounder' had been used in a 1970s Australian schoolyard. The point of the story – other than my particular idiocy – is the way I was so fully engaged in that other world at the moment of intrusion. We don't talk about 'getting lost in a book' for nothing. I was completely locked away with Bertie, Jeeves, Gussie Fink-Nottle and the various doings at the Drones Club, and no longer twelve and pimply and alienated and – can this list get any bleaker? – oh, that's right, living in Canberra.

Are there any hardcore readers who had happy childhoods? Was there ever a person ensconced in the in crowd – invited to play football in the First XV; asked to captain both the netball team and the social committee – who said, 'No, actually, I have some reading to do'? Was reading only ever the escape hatch for those of us with no better options?

Since I'm sitting at a literary festival, I keep these thoughts to myself. I look at the people around me; a sea of bookish faces. Do we all share some secret misery that led us here? Maybe it's a good sign that my son has never been a reader. He has had other options. We protected him from vicious dogs. He never had asthma. His mother has yet to run off.

At the end of the weekend I drive home, thinking about my own relationship with reading. It is true I first opened the trapdoor because I was looking to escape a somewhat tricky place. Once inside, though, there were whole landscapes to explore, each place leading to another, endlessly engrossing, rewarding, consoling.

Every reader knows about the strange time-travelling ability of books. The local library, we realised early, was the cheapest travel agent in town. Sometimes a place visited in a book stayed in the memory more vividly than a place visited physically. I am hazy on the Hong Kong I visited in 1989 or the Hobart of 2001, but I can easily direct you around the London of 1974, which I toured on the arm of Hanif Kureishi, or Levin's snowbound farm in Russia, as mapped by Leo Tolstoy.

Most readers will have an experience like this – of books creating an escape hatch into another world. It can't be chance that some of our most treasured books feature a literal escape hatch: the *Narnia* books, the *Magic Faraway Tree*, even *Dr Who* make explicit the process of tumbling into a new world.

Occasionally, I am still overcome by the opportunity of reading, the pure good fortune of it. Given a computer or a well-stocked bookshelf, you could be sitting with Plato within a few minutes of reading this sentence. Just the two of you, as intimate as that sounds. Or tramping the Hindu Kush with Eric Newby. Or driving through Middle America with Anne Tyler.

More than that, reading is an answer to the narcissism of our time. Social media, of course, has many good points, especially the way it allows you to form communities outside the limitations of your own location. Yet Facebook and Twitter create a sense that you're at the centre of a universe of your own creation; you're the planet around which everything swirls – your friends, your tastes, your hobbies. It's as if we've reverted to a pre-Copernican world, creating a universe with ourselves at the centre. Yet, as every teenager knows, ego always seems to travel hand-in-hand with self-doubt, and time spent staring appreciatively into the mirror almost always turns sour.

That's the strange thing about self-love: it's so rarely reciprocated.

Reading offers a universe that doesn't revolve around us – our problems, our vanities and our fears. In Tolstoy's *Anna Karenina*, there's a scene when Anna's child has been taken away by the husband she spurned. She's heartbroken and wants to tell her lover, Vronsky, about how terrible she feels. She pauses, worried about the look of disdain she knows will pass over Vronsky's face should she unburden herself. Once she's seen that dismissive look, she'll find it impossible to love him. And so she says nothing.

By this stage in the story, she's a character we don't even like; yet the reader is overwhelmed with sympathy. You feel like cradling Anna in your arms. In that one scene – it's only a few lines of text – we understand the extent of what she has given up; how little she will receive in return; and – here's the painful bit – that she knows all this herself.

This is what fiction does, encouraging us to see the world through the eyes of someone else; in Anna's case, a person from a different country and century. It's a masterclass in empathy.

The library and the bookshop are, if you like, gymnasiums of empathy. And by training our empathy muscles, reading changes the world.

I might have been brought to the trapdoor by some momentary pain, but I now understand it was worth it. What's asthma and abandonment if it leads to Hilary Mantel, Thea Astley, and the newspaper columns of Alan Coren?

When I get home my son is still on the couch, reading. He has downloaded most of Conan Doyle and stares, entranced by the words. I feel my heart skip in delight.

Oh joy. Maybe he had bad parents and a miserable childhood after all.

The Mother Tongue

There's a good argument that the world's mothers are not as nice as they seem. Here's a list of all the things that mothers say to their children – and what they really mean.

- *Mummy and Daddy are going to have an afternoon rest.* Mummy and Daddy are going to attempt to have sex for the first time since, let me count, 1947.
- *It really is bedtime.* I've just downloaded *Game of Thrones* and there's a bottle of wine chilling in the freezer.
- *Too much cake will rot your teeth.* I was rather hoping to eat the rest of that cake myself.
- *Go and play in the lovely sunshine.* Five more minutes in your company and I'll be arrested for murder.
- *If you eat your greens you will be big and strong.* If you don't eat your greens, you'll eat biscuits instead and suffer a hyperactivity meltdown about 6.25pm, when I can least endure it.

- *Daddy is just having a little rest.* Daddy is passed out, pissed, on the nature strip.
- *And that's the end of the lovely picture book!* Funny how quickly it goes when you surreptitiously turn over five pages at a time.
- *You look such a big boy in that jacket.* It's a hand-me-down from a thirteen-year-old cousin, which is why it's trailing the ground like an old man's dressing gown.
- *Lots of big boys wear pink.* It's a hand-me-down from your five-year-old sister and even she found it effeminate.
- *It's fun to have your hair cut by your mother.* With the $23 I save I can buy gin.
- *Once you're asleep you'll have lovely sweet dreams.* Once you're asleep Mummy and Daddy are breaking open the Sara Lee Chocolate Bavarian.
- *We're nearly home.* Daddy's lost.
- *Daddy is just going on a little walk to the next town.* Daddy forgot to fill the petrol tank.
- *We're going to have a special adventure and all sleep in the car.* Daddy forgot to book somewhere to stay.
- *It was amazing when you kicked the soccer ball right past the goalie.* Next time, try kicking it into the other team's goal. You may find it somewhat more difficult.
- *Next time we come, we can spend as long as you like saying hello to the monkeys and the*

seals. We're never coming to the zoo again, not after the blood transfusion your father required once he'd paid for the tickets.

- *The Mr Whippy man is playing 'Greensleeves', which means he's run out of ice-cream.* If you believe that, you'll believe anything.
- *There's a rule at Woolworths that people with children are not allowed to purchase biscuits.* If you believe that, you'll believe anything.
- *But Mummy and Daddy can't afford to buy a whole bottle of fizzy drink.* Have you seen the price of gin?
- *You'll get a better sound from your violin if you practise in the garage.* With the stereo turned up really high I may be able to avoid the confronting sound of your complete lack of talent.
- *Don't be silly, the dentist doesn't hurt.* He hasn't hurt Mummy or Daddy, since we've assiduously avoided check-ups for the last twenty years.
- *What a lovely surprise – chocolates for Mother's Day.* Not that much of a surprise, actually, since I pre-ordered them at the chocolate shop, gave your father the money and waited in the car while he picked them up.
- *You look tired.* I feel tired.
- *You've too much on to have Sam over to play.* Sam is a bad seed who will tempt you down the path of misbehaviour and evil, resulting in you both becoming heroin addicts and convicted thieves by the time you are thirteen.

- *I think Sam is busy anyway.* That child is not entering this home unless I'm armed with plastic sheeting and a gun.
- *Look, I'm dialling Sam's house now and there's no answer.* The Taxis Combined voice-recognition service is quite confused by what I'm saying.
- *What do you mean you've rung Sam's mother on my mobile and they are on their way over?* Where's that bottle of gin?

And, drum roll, please:
- *This is the last time I'll say this.* Over the next fifteen years I'll say this another 4.3 million times.

The Decade of the Busted Bidet

When you are growing up, you study your own parents, as well as the parents of your friends, and assume everything they do is normal and reasonable. Now, looking back, it's clear they were all insane.

For a start, every family in the 1970s had a chest freezer for reasons I still don't quite understand. It's not that we didn't have butchers; the place was awash in fresh meat. Yet, according to our collective parents, we wanted no part in its purchase. The go was to buy fifty kilos of meat every six months and store it in an inconveniently large freezer placed against the back wall of the garage, as if you were living on a remote island reliant on passing shipping, and not in a suburban bungalow over the road from Woolworths.

The meat tasted terrible, you had to remember to thaw out a portion or two every morning, and the freezer took up so much of the garage the car had to be left in the street. Despite all this, no one questioned the hegemony of the freezer-to-plate system.

Perhaps people were too busy to shop. After all,

the nation was flat-out learning speed-reading. Speed-reading, much like polio, has now been eradicated in most of the First World, but back then everyone believed that reading *War and Peace* in two and half hours was an excellent way to pick up its many nuances. In fact, bookshops in the 1970s consisted of little else other than books on speed reading. No one thought to ask the obvious question: if speed-reading works so well, how come no one had time to read anything other than books on speed-reading?

It was not the only obvious question to go unasked. The purchase of soda water, for example, was deemed a luxury too great for most families. You had to make your own. Each family invested in a soda syphon, a large device fashioned from brushed aluminium in which you inserted a carbon dioxide bulb, bought at considerable expense. The soda would come out either completely flat or in such an explosive burst that it would knock the glass from your hand. Nonetheless, the elaborate process – together with the presence of this much-brushed aluminium – lent an air of sophistication to a night getting hammered on Scotch and soda.

Such drunkenness posed dangers when it came time to carve the leg of lamb, dragged some hours earlier from the chest freezer and then cooked until ruined. A carving knife was considered a poor choice. Instead an electric knife was employed, the duel blades of which sawed back and forth, drowning out the conversation, splattering the diners with food scraps and tearing the meat to shreds. The device would then slice through its own electrical cord, plunging the house into darkness. Ask people why they employed this method and they'd reply: 'It's more glamorous.'

It was the same search for glamour which led to the great bidet boom of 1974, in which French-style bum-washers were installed in every Australian bathroom. The next year they were all removed, along with Gough Whitlam and his ministers, after people realised they didn't know what they were for. (The bidets, not the ministers.)

The bidet, for some unknown reason, was seen as sexy and thus connected with the free love movement of the 1960s. The movement only reached the Australian suburbs in a modified form – rather like a cyclone which has degenerated into a tropical depression. What had been a case of sex, drugs and rock 'n' roll in Paris, London and New York emerged a decade later in Australia as the odd game of Twister with some folks from round the corner.

Twister, however, did give the opportunity for Barry from number 6 to press his thigh against the elbow of Susan from number 3. Having achieved that level of physical intimacy, they would then be in a position to jointly marvel at the bidet John and Barbara had just installed in the ensuite bathroom, exclaiming 'What's it for?', 'How does it work?' and 'What happens if I sit down and press this button?' as they waited for the arrival of a fresh bottle of Liebfraumilch.

The young people of the time would cower at the top of the stairs, or perhaps peep through their fingers, hoping the horror would stop. In the end it did. The chest freezers were thrown on the dump, alongside a million busted bidets. The Twister mat was put away amid allegations that Tina in number 7 had fallen pregnant with twins after a particularly tangled encounter with Noel from number 11. And the glamour of electrical kitchen appliances began to wane, even unto the point where the electric knife was slipped quietly into the second drawer down.

Only then could we, the young people of the 1970s, emerge from our hidey-holes and face the world. A terrible darkness had engulfed the nation but we had survived. Blinking against the light, we determined to try and build a better world, one fresh chop, and one slowly savoured book, at a time.

Catcher in the Fry

J.D. Salinger may have been one of the world's greatest writers, yet he took time out from his work to praise Burger King's flame-grilled Whopper burger. It was 'better than just edible', he wrote in a letter recently released – and certainly far superior to the burgers offered by other establishments.

If Salinger – Zen Buddhist recluse and intellectual – could gain such pleasure from a Whopper, it raises the question: are there other oft-derided aspects of ordinary life deserving of a little more praise?

Instant coffee, for example. Who, amid the coffee Nazism of our time, would dare admit that instant coffee is a fairly decent drink? The typical Australian workplace is now full of crazed coffee zealots who feel the need to lecture you for hours about the differences between *this* cafe and *that* cafe and their preference for a macchiato as opposed to a double-shot espresso with ristretto tendencies. Really? How interesting. Tell me more.

Actually don't say that or they will, filling you in on the employment history of their favourite barista with the sort of hushed reverence once reserved for a saint. When this particular barista has a day off, the whole office falls into a slough of despond, with people wondering aloud whether they will be able to face the challenges of the day ahead without the succour provided by one of Michael's flat whites.

They should have a cup of instant and get on with it.

The truth is that instant coffee costs a few cents a cup and most of the time tastes better than the bitter, dirty brew slopped into your cup via the clogged pipes of some ill-managed high street machine. Better still, the cheaper the brand of instant coffee, the better the flavour. Oh, for a cup of Pablo topped with a spoonful of sugar and a glug of full-cream milk. Enjoy in moderation and don't admit to your colleagues how delicious it is.

I'd also like to see more praise for Australian tap water – a product even more ubiquitous than the Whopper. Much of the world lacks decent drinking water. We have it piped into home and office and yet insist on buying plastic bottles of the stuff.

Since when did a walk in the park necessitate constant drinking or, as it is now called, 'hydration'? Watch people on the Bondi to Bronte walk and you'd think they were attempting a crossing of the Serengeti. Some have several bottles of the stuff and take a sip every three steps as if their bodies are buckets with holes in the bottom through which a stream of water constantly gushes. The bubbler doesn't appear to provide a solution. That would involve just drinking the stuff; their ambition is to 'hydrate'.

Will a future generation of Australian children, calling from their rooms at bedtime, no longer demand 'a glass of water, please, Daddy', but instead shriek, 'Mummy, quick, quick. I need rehydrating'? And since bottled water didn't really exist twenty years ago, can someone explain how humans survived up to this point? Did we just stay at home, tethered to the tap, unable to venture outside lest we fall into a thirst-induced coma within a few steps of the front door? Or did office workers and shoppers wander down Main Street African-style, a yoke thrown across their shoulders with a bucket of water sloshing around on each side?

The home-cooked meal also deserves more praise. Restaurant chefs claim to be obsessed with 'fresh ingredients simply prepared', but they never follow through. Everything is presented in little towers, as if the plate was valuable real estate. It's then splashed with a mélange of butter, cream and salt in a way designed to cause a heart attack. The only place you actually get 'fresh ingredients simply prepared' is at home. A chop, mashed potatoes and some steamed beans. Maybe Terry Durack could come around to your place and describe just how fantastic it tastes.

Cask wine also needs rehabilitation; it's seen far too much criticism over the years, depicted as the 'Broadmeadows briefcase' or 'the goon sack'. The contents might be unremarkable but there are definite benefits: the price is good, the packaging allows you to fool yourself about how much you are drinking, and the silver bladder inside provides either a makeshift disco ball or an excellent pillow, depending on the progress of the party. Really, it's not so much a drink as a complete party kit.

Once we admit the Whopper tastes pretty good, we may have to reconsider many of the other things we've spent the past few decades deriding. Domestic beer? Frankly, it's much better than the imported stuff, which is stale by the time it gets here. A kebab from the local shops? Let's face it: magnificent. Network television? It can be relaxing after a long day at work.

The virtues of the ordinary and the every day? Maybe Salinger was on to something.

The Beard Boom

The whole young-man beard thing is out of control. Even that nice Joe O'Brien from ABC News 24 looks like something from a 'Wanted' poster. There you are watching the prime minister being interviewed and the guy asking the questions appears to be a Mexican bandit. You half-expect the camera to pull back to reveal two sharpshooters, an ammunition strap and a mariachi band.

Out on the streets every man under the age of twenty-five has a beard. And not just a tufty arty affair. They are going for the full bushranger look: big, glossy productions that tumble from the face like a hairy waterfall. Most young men now look as if you've caught them midway through eating a fox, the rear end of the animal still trying to wriggle free.

It's the most baffling male fashion trend since the natty little hat epidemic of late 2009.

Who knows how they've managed to grow them so fast. Yesterday they were all clean-shaven. Today it's Rasputin city. Perhaps their facial hair has responded to global warming in the same way as my lawn. Or, like me, have they overdone the Weed 'n' Feed?

I stand back in admiration. They possess more testosterone than I enjoyed at their age. When I was in my twenties, I had so few chest hairs I awarded them individual names. Veronica, Charlotte and Suzie. It was a measly crop, easily mistaken for eczema. Only after a lot of praying and breath holding did I manage to give them some company. Naturally I never considered a beard. Not only was I unequal to the task, I found them a little repulsive. People were messy eaters in those days. The typical bearded man could live for a week on the food caught in his hedge. It was more a mobile larder than a fashion statement.

Women, by and large, weren't keen on having a relationship with a bearded man. Just kissing him was like rooting around in the small goods section of your local supermarket. You never knew when you'd emerge with a chunk of salami well past its use-by date. There was also a suggestion that those with beards had something to hide, the most common allegation being possession of 'a weak chin'. Presumably the bigger the beard, the weaker the chin, right up to Ned Kelly whose chin, under this theory, was so weak it had to be covered with a beard plus a metal mask made of old ploughs.

Some women also claimed the bearded man was less than ideal during lovemaking. A candlelit hour with a bearded man could, they reported, leave you feeling like you'd spent time pashing a belt sander. The point was strenuously denied by the bearded men, who described the experience as 'like being caressed by angel wings', a phrase their partners disputed as 'inaccurate bordering on delusional'.

So what's happened to change the landscape? Why have the young men of Australia embraced the bearded life? Could it be a response to the achievements of feminism? The embittered older man – okay, for the sake of ease let's call him 'Alan Jones' – whinges about women being in power, claiming they have 'destroyed the joint'. The younger man merely shrugs his shoulders and says, 'We're happy to join hands with Australia's women in this world of equality. I'm not emasculated ... I mean, look at *this*.' His hands indicate the beard, in all its hirsute glory.

Who wouldn't be happy to share political and economic power when their body thrums with such masculinity? It's just their way of saying, 'Go ahead, run stuff, I'll be getting on with growing *the magnificence*.'

More likely still, it's a response to changes in the workplace. In the old days we'd shave and wear a tie to prove to the boss that we were tamed and under his control: 'See here, I've passed a razor over my face to remove any sign of my animal heritage, plus I've placed this floral noose around my neck to indicate that I am tethered and in your control at all times. If I do anything wrong, I'll be very easy to strangle; just hold the knot here and pull down hard on the thin end.'

On weekends, we'd remove the tie and not shave for a day in a vain attempt to reassert our masculinity. In extreme cases we'd skip having a shower. None of that works now the weekend no longer exists. In the world of email, mobile phones and social media, the boss controls all your time. It's hardly surprising that, in response, there's a small act of defiance: no more ties and a flourishing of big, bushy beards.

It's just a way of saying, 'You may have my testicles in your hand, boss, but notice that the harder you squeeze, the bigger the crop that grows up here.'

Of course, in the modern workplace there's also no time to leave your desk for lunch. How lucky, with a beard, you always have some spare food on hand.

The World's Most Annoying Phrases

There's a scene in one of Julian Barnes's novels where the main character spots the phrase 'hand-cut chips' on a pub menu. He asks if his chips can be cut a little thinner than the ones he sees around him. As Barnes puts it, 'the barman's normal affableness took a pause'. Slowly, painfully, the reality is communicated: 'hand-cut' doesn't mean the chips are in any way cut by hand. It means they are machine cut and supplied frozen in a bag, just like everything else. The 'hand-cut' means they are thick-style chips, which is why it makes no sense to ask for them cut thin.

Put like that, 'hand-cut chips' is pretty annoying, but it's not the only contender for the world's most annoying phrase. Voting is now open on these:

'Stop screaming, Tiffany'
I am full of sympathy for parents whose children are having a meltdown in the supermarket. And, certainly,

I agree that Tiffany should stop screaming. Everyone in the supermarket and in adjoining shops agrees that Tiffany should stop screaming. The message, though, needs to be delivered to Tiffany. Instead it's delivered upwards and outwards to the rest of us as if to say, 'I know! She's a real shocker! You think you're enduring hell. I have to spend all day with her!'

'Just sayin''

If you use this phrase on Twitter you are a malevolent troll who is trying to somehow pretend that being abusive is cute and hip. Well, it's not. Just sayin'.

'Minister, with respect ...'

Why does this phrase always precede the point in the interview at which the least respect is shown? 'Minister, with respect, you lied, and know you lied, and we know you lied.' How is that 'with respect'? Was there an alternative approach, which the interviewer was actively considering, of asking that same question but with even less respect? Was she planning to fart at the same time as the question was being put, so as to vividly indicate the ordure in which the government was steeped? Was she considering pulling a face or chundering into a bucket to vividly illustrate the contempt she was feeling at the time?

It's the only way to make sense of the phrase: she was going to do all that, then decided to hold back. Thus the formulation: 'Minister, with respect ...'

*

'I feel humbled'

This is the phrase people always use after they've won an award. Why, at this point, should you feel humbled? Here's the dictionary definition of 'humbled': 'to make somebody feel less proud or convinced of his or her own ability or importance'. Imagine how the organisers of the award must feel. They've searched through thousands of possibilities, selected you as the best in your field, held a glittering awards ceremony and, as a result of all of that, you say you feel less self-confident than you did yesterday. You feel less capable? Less important?

If people really did feel humbled when they won, surely we would have to do away with awards altogether, since they would result in a perpetual crisis of confidence among our best and brightest, leaving in their wake shattered people, unable to continue the very work that brought them to the award podium in the first place. Thank goodness it's all rubbish and they are only using the word 'humbled' in a vain attempt to hide the way their brain is loudly playing the theme to *Rocky*.

'I just have to grab some butter'

This is said with a small apologetic grimace and a 'silly me' shrug of the shoulders by the man in front of you in the checkout queue as he darts away, leaving $200 worth of shopping between you and any hope of escaping the supermarket this calendar year. 'I'll only be a second,' he calls back as he scampers off, heading up aisle five, which everyone knows is the wrong aisle, leaving you and the checkout chap staring bleakly at each other while the heavens spin and autumn turns into winter, the ice caps melt and the sun exhausts itself and dims to just a faint glow in the sky. 'Sorry,' he says brightly on his return. 'I didn't know whether we wanted salted or unsalted, so I had to ring home.' Surely eighteen years in Long Bay Jail would be worth the pleasure of killing him, right here, right now, with the sharp end of his toilet duck as the weapon.

'He's perfectly friendly'

This is the phrase gaily shouted across the park as you look up to see forty-five kilograms of American pit bull terrier hurtling towards you, possibly airborne, slobber coming off in sheets, jaws open, growling constantly, like the drone of an incoming missile, in a trajectory that suggests you are about to lose your left testicle. True, the dog eventually slows down and merely snaps at your leg in a way that could be described as 'friendly' if your point of comparison is being eaten alive by lions. You might even bend over to pat the beast, were it not for a left testicle that has now retracted so far into your body it might never re-emerge. 'You see!' trills the owner as the dog loses interest in the immediate consumption of your body parts. 'I told you he was friendly.'

'I only had one bruschetta and the cheapest main course'

This is said the moment the bill is delivered to the table of twenty, and already the guy has his calculator out and is offering to handle the money 'as it's only fair that people pay for what they had'. As you say your goodbyes, you note he drives off in a Mercedes convertible.

'Made the traditional way'
This phrase is normally accompanied by a picture of an older woman in a shawl, as if the 50,000 meat pies sold in Colesworth each week were all produced by a briskly efficient woman called Auntie Vera in the back of her Federation cottage just outside Braidwood or Bright in the hour or so before church each Sunday, rather than in a large steel vat by poorly paid guest workers in a vermin-infested industrial estate in Moorebank or Moorabbin. An identical-looking woman is pictured on nearly all the packets in the supermarket – pies, jams, biscuits and frozen lasagnes – so it's little wonder the illustration shows a few wisps of hair have escaped her bonnet. The poor dear must be flat out.

'Fat-free'
Well, yes, it is fat-free, that's true. The complication is that it's a bottle of cordial, a product that doesn't normally contain fat. So why pretend it's a health food when the real issue is not the fat but the sugar and your particular product contains half Queensland's annual crop mixed with a jigger of cancer-causing chemicals? Ditto 'sugar-free' on products that would never conceivably contain sugar, as if soon they'll be advertising DVD players and garden rakes with 'no added calories', and undies and light-bulbs as 'low-carb'. Why not have a new advertising slogan: a little circle saying 'falsehood-free' in which you

abstain from advertising the absence of things you'd never expect to be present.

'We just sold the last one'
No, you didn't. You've been out of stock for months. In fact, you've probably never stocked it. And even if, by some freakish chance, you just served the only other person in town who, this bright Saturday morning, was in search of a rear-fitting grommet-buckler, why do you suppose it will make me feel better to know that, had I been five minutes earlier, victory would have been mine? Just tell me the truth: 'We don't stock it. We've never stocked it, I don't know where you can get one, and, actually, I haven't the foggiest what you are talking about.'

'We're making some exciting changes to your credit card at no extra cost to you as part of our ongoing commitment to providing value to our customers'
This lengthy phrase comes in written form, presented on your bank's letterhead and signed by some fictional executive with a pleasant-sounding name such as Jasmine Peters or Michelle Sweetpea. Enclosed with the perky letter is a 144-page brochure of impenetrable legalese, printed in eight-point type, providing what are called 'some extra details you should know about the changes'. This is like the moment the school bully turns and smiles and pretends to be friendly. You just know something really bad is about to happen, even though the exact nature of the coming horror remains hard to predict.

'It must be a problem with your router'

Every computer system has three or four elements – computer, router, modem, internet provider. This means that the problem is never the fault of the company into whose call centre you have rung, enduring a six-hour wait, during which time you have heard Vivaldi's *Four Seasons* so many times that you've taken to mumbling 'this is the winter of our discontent' whenever it gets to the fourth movement. Each call ends with the suggestion you phone someone else, with the helpful provision of the number of the router company or the modem man or the service provider, at which point you get to enjoy another sixteen hours of Vivaldi and being told 'your call is important to us' so many times you want to bludgeon yourself into unconsciousness. This is when the call is finally answered, you are pretty sure, by the same young man in the same Indian call centre, which has, you later discover, a contract with all four companies.

'What do you offer for the advanced child?'

This is asked in a tone of concerned entitlement, just as the school's parent information night winds its way tantalisingly close to its finish, as if this particular parent didn't ask for a gifted child, but that's her lot in life, especially since being as talented as her Samantha is virtually a disability and should therefore be resourced accordingly. If her child really needs extending, I'd suggest breadcrumbs, mixed with a little sage ...

'This is just a courtesy call ...'

No it's not. What's courtesy got to do with it? This phrase is either used by telemarketers who have just rung in the middle of dinner or your hairdresser seeking to confirm your appointment so they won't be left with an unproductive gap on a Tuesday afternoon. This is fair enough but hardly Sir Walter Raleigh throwing his cape over a puddle so the Queen's feet stay dry. The rule is simple: anyone who uses the word 'courtesy' should not be trying to make their own life easier.

'You'll need to speak to Darren and he's on a flex day'

It's always Darren and he's always on a flex day. Is Darren actually a mythical figure – a creature created by office workers so they can palm off queries too complicated to answer? When a company has cash-flow problems, does it have recourse to a 'Darren' who must be contacted before any cheques can be signed? And are there people who really are called Darren who have to change their names in order not to be lumbered with the 23,000 calls banked up for the official 'Darren' whose flex days shall last forever?

Of course, in the contest for the world's most annoying phrase, there are plenty more contenders. I'd ask Darren to jot down some further suggestions but he's just flexed off.

Chapter 4

In which all women are found to be beautiful and a First World problem is encountered

First World Problem

I have a problem with my dishwasher but there's no point telling anyone. Whenever I do, hoping for a little sympathy, the person I'm addressing smiles, leans closer and then, with a twinkle in the eye, says, 'First World problem.'

The phrase 'First World problem' is the 'hump day' of our time. It is the '24/7' or the 'as you do' of today: a phrase that's all over town like a cheap shirt. It's usually said with a rising intonation of merry dismay that should be represented by an exclamation mark or two, so it's really 'First World problem!!'

The tone spells out the message: for me even to mention my malfunctioning dishwasher is to actively ignore the plight of the several billion in the world who dream not only of a dishwasher, but of a sink; not only of a sink, but of any sort of vessel containing potable water. Fair enough point, I guess, but some people seem to add a third or fourth exclamation mark – 'First World problem!!!!' – as if I have personally gone and punctured the only water pipe to the driest village in Africa.

So, repeat after me: 'I must stop whingeing about my dishwasher, even if it no longer washes dishes.'

The problem is I live a First World life. What other problems am I going to have, other than First World ones? Even if I develop a life-threatening illness, or my relationship breaks up, or I catch my penis in the zip of my pants – all things that can happen in any of the worlds – the drama will be played out in ways particular to the world in which I'm residing.

In this case, the dishwasher must be serviced by the dishwasher man, who must visit the house when someone is home, but that's *never*, because here in the First World most of us leave the house to go to work each day, and while you could stay home one morning if you knew in advance they were coming, the dishwasher people won't allow you to make a time-specific appointment, since they appear to be under the misapprehension that it is still 1953 and every house comes equipped with a live-in maid, although they will ring you the night before and tell you the time they intend coming and allow you to cancel the appointment if the time doesn't suit.

'I'll have to cancel.'

'We have another available next Tuesday.'

'Morning or afternoon?'

'As usual, we'll tell you the night before. If it doesn't suit, you can cancel.'

This means you have to make a series of appointments, all of them days ahead, each of which you have to cancel once it's clear they intend coming at a time you can't be there.

It's at this point, after two weeks of intense appointment-making and appointment-breaking, each failed rendezvous edging me closer to pulsating, knife-wielding, mouth-frothing insanity, that in answer to the query 'How are you?' I occasionally mumble: 'Not too good, actually. Dishwasher problems ...'

Cue friend/colleague/stranger on stairs: 'First World problem!!!!'

In every human heart there's a mix of happiness and despair, often achieved whatever the external circumstances. One person can win the lottery and another lose a leg, but often the leg loser is happier than the lottery winner, which is just one of those strange and glorious things about life. Or, to put it another way: in each life some rain must fall.

First World problems? I have a few.

There are so many devices connected to our television that watching the news involves fifteen minutes of rooting around at the back of the set, followed by ten minutes restarting the T-Box – 'Where did I write down the password?' – and five minutes repeatedly hitting the 'source' button in an attempt to get something vaguely resembling Juanita Phillips to appear. To watch the 7pm news, I now find it sensible to begin my preparations at 6pm.

More? The seams on my new Ted Baker pants are pulling apart in the bum area – my fault for buying them one size too small. My subscription to the *Sunday Times* no longer works because I have a first-generation iPad. And the poor industrial design of our fridge means that every time you sling the milk onto the top shelf, it hits the temperature knob and everything freezes.

Yet into this thicket of First World misery, some sunshine must come. The dishwasher man finally picks a time when I can be home. He arrives. He is pleasant. He is skilful. He removes some panels and summons me over. Cradled in his hand are a few shards of glass. 'Here's your problem. They were stuck in the mechanism.'

As he shows me the fragments, I recall what happened. I'd broken a wine glass while putting it in the dishwasher; this on an evening on which I'd drunk too much of my current favourite, a rather cheeky Mudgee semillon ($16.99 a bottle, if you must know).

I feel like presenting my wrists so I can be handcuffed. 'Fair cop, gov. You've got me fair and square.' *Fine stemware broken by a tipsy Westerner attempting to use an expensive appliance after drinking too much posh grog?* 'First World problem!!!!!!'

All that's left is for me to be dragged to a prison cell constructed entirely of exclamation marks so I can quietly contemplate my crimes.

Dark Ages

The council in the Welsh city of Cardiff has installed yellow lighting at selected spots to prevent teenagers from congregating. The coloured lighting highlights their pimples, making them look unattractive. Thus, they move on. This may seem unfair on the young, until you realise the rest of the world has been busy installing equipment that moves on middle-aged people in just the same way.

Why else have they ripped the carpets and curtaining from every restaurant so the whole place becomes an echoing box in which it's impossible for anybody over twenty-five to have a conversation?

One realises that people in their forties and fifties are unattractive, our teeth failing to sparkle as we bite into the bocconcini and our hair refusing to glint in the sunlight as we lean back in our chair to laugh at the bon mot about Gotye just dropped by our Campari-swilling companion. But our money is good. Couldn't they find a little curtained room out the back in which we could sit quietly and eat our meal? We'd be happy for something on a tray, which we could eat on our laps, nursing-home style.

Instead, we sit amid the artfully achieved cacophony, perched upright and attentive at the table like startled meerkats, trying to catch a single word spoken by our companions. The other night I had dinner with a school friend who has been appointed president of Tanzania. Or possibly he's moving to Tasmania. Certainly it started with a T.

The young may wonder why the middle-aged are often short of friends. It's because we've nodded, smiled and said, 'Wonderful news' over a restaurant table after our chum inaudibly revealed that her mother died that very morning.

Meanwhile the whole experience of shopping is now designed to enrage and confuse all but the very young. Wandering around Melbourne's CBD during my Christmas holidays, I investigated some bargain T-shirts only to discover that the one I liked was stained.

'Do you have one of these T-shirts without the stain?' I asked the young man behind the counter. He frowned, puzzled, wondering how to explain.

'It's not really a stain,' he said, as I held the T-shirt for inspection.

'Look here,' I said, showing the patch of darker dye in the spot where a pocket might normally go.

'It's designed to be there,' he said and paused, still searching for the words. 'The idea is that this is an old, favourite T-shirt, one you've had for years, so old that the pocket has fallen off, so there's a darker patch where the pocket used to be.'

He smiled helpfully.

'You mean,' I said, 'the pocket that was never there.'

'Yes, but the pocket that would have been there, had there been a pocket, which then fell off because you wore the shirt too much.'

I don't know how much they are paying this chap but it's not enough. The T-shirt in my hand was so complex in its conceptual underpinnings it should come complete with an integrated essay by Roland Barthes.

As I stood there I found myself wondering how they explain the phantom pocket to the Chinese workers who make this stuff.

'So, let me get this right,' says the foreman at the No. 1 factory in Shenzhen. 'You want the T-shirt to look as if we made it so badly that it had a pocket but then the pocket fell off.'

'Well, kind of. Yes.'

'It would be easier for us to just add a pocket. Then you'd have a pocket. Useful for putting things in.'

'We don't want a pocket.'

'That, too, is easy. We will make it without a pocket.'

'No, we want it to look as if it had a pocket early on.'

In the foetid atmosphere of the non air-conditioned factory, the men are left staring at each other in mutually assured incomprehension.

Back in the Melbourne shopping mall, I smiled and handed over my money. 'I'll have two of them,'

I announced, and the nice young man wrapped them up – two T-shirts identically stained by the pocket that never was.

I'm happy enough with my purchase: on the down side, the phantom pockets prove Western society has collapsed into madness; on the other hand, the neckline rather suits me.

I take my parcel and move rapidly on. Wandering the streets, I attempt to buy a pair of pants to go with my new stained T-shirts. It's pretty much impossible. For the over-thirties the windows of most shops provide little more than a shouted instruction to move on. Much like what's happened to the kids of Cardiff with their illuminated pimples.

And so today we link arms in opposition to age-based oppression in all its guises. Comrades, will you join me?

Facebook Faux Pas

Here's a list of the Twenty Worst Facebook Faux Pas, only half of which have been committed by me.

1. Supplying too much information. We're all happy your sex life is good. After twenty years of marriage, that's fabulous. It's lovely to think a couple in their fifties can be so creative and, well, flexible. The photo, though, is too much.

2. Speaking about yourself in the third person. 'Diane is hopeful'; 'Diane wants a better world'; 'Diane is contemplating a trip to the bathroom'. Speaking about oneself in the third person should be left to those most experienced at the art: sports stars and politicians.

3. Posting unhappy status updates such as 'Sad' or 'Bad news' without explanation, forcing everyone to ask 'Why?' or 'Please tell us what's wrong'.

4. Posting happy status updates such as 'Thrilling news' or 'I can't believe my luck' without explanation, forcing everyone to ask 'Why?' or 'Please tell us what happened'.

5. Bragging. The phrase is 'status update', not 'socio-economic status update', so why the constant showing off, as in 'First trip in my new BMW' or 'First day as managing director' or 'Off to Whistler, skiing'?

6. Bragging by proxy. Signing up to the *Guardian*'s Facebook app and then clicking on all the posh articles, just so your friends will receive the notification: 'Justin Kington recently read the article "God Particles and their role in the ontology of Julian Assange".' We know the truth: a full log of what you've been reading on the internet would not look so pretty.

7. Setting up a Facebook page in the name of your dog and then inviting people to 'friend' it. The constant status updates – 'Just had din-dins', 'Sleeping now' and the hilarious 'Woof' – are not helping.

8. Being insensitive to the dangers of the word 'like'. Yes, on Facebook it's a way of saying you've read something and appreciate knowing the information. Yet the phrase 'Bill O'Brien likes this' doesn't look so good printed below the status update: 'My partner just got sacked'.

9. Posting a blow-by-blow account of that night's TV viewing in which you neglect to include the name of the shows you are watching, as in 'He's just entirely lost the argument', 'No crime suspect would be that stupid' and 'A politician wearing that shirt! LOL'. It may come as a shock

but not everyone is involved in the same activity as you.

10. Using LOL.

11. Syncing your Twitter account to your Facebook page so your Facebook friends find themselves wading through one side of a conversation, already incomprehensible, but made more so by a confetti of @s and #s.

12. Using @ in a FB message because you think Twitter is cool.

13. Adding someone's name to a group in which they could have no conceivable interest. I'm sure the Sutherland Carpool Club is a noble institution but do I need to be notified of its every move? Yes, I know I could block it. I haven't got around to it yet.

14. Including everyone in your FarmVille updates so we're all told you've been awarded a Masters in Broccoli and paid a neighbour to unwither your pumpkins. Yes, I know I could block it. I haven't got around to it yet.

15. Tagging an image – such as a flyer for your band – as if it contains photos of all your friends. The idea is that every time anyone comments on the image, everyone on the list is sent a message saying 'Laura Perkins just commented on a photo of you', which then forces them to look. This is not marketing; it's mugging.

16. Having an endless argument on someone else's page, especially about a subject in which the

page-owner has no real interest. For example: the Meryl Streep fan who mentions her wonderful performance as Margaret Thatcher, only to find herself hosting a 120-post row between fifteen people she's never heard of about the rights and wrongs of the 1984–85 British miners' strike.

17. Completing a quiz on 'Which Roman monarch are you?' or 'Which dairy-based dessert are you?' or 'If you were a prostitute what sort of prostitute would you be?' and then sending it to everyone you know.

18. Sending a private message about your business to your entire friend list so people think they have an exciting private message, or even an intriguing ten private messages, only to find it's actually a bit of advertising, which ten people have commented on, most of the comments being: 'Stop sending me this crap'.

19. Posting any photo of me – or anyone else – on holidays when I am wearing garish shorts, have an unattractively sunburnt nose and a holiday beer-belly. 'Do unto others' as the Bible presciently put it – and that's despite being published before Facebook was even invented.

20. Posting a link to your own work or an archive of your own work just so you'll get more hits. An example would be me posting a link to richardglover.com.au – and as if I'd ever do something as pathetic and self-serving as that.

Virtually Amish

Three weeks ago I read the latest study on mobile phones and decided they may be unsafe. Since then, I've limited use of my mobile, disconnected the cordless phone, and begun to worry about our wi-fi. At this rate, I'll be Amish by the end of the month.

I've replaced the cordless with an old-fashioned corded phone, complete with fifteen metres of cabling so people can take the phone wherever they want in the house. The cord lies in a series of tangled heaps along the hallway floor like fallen bunting.

Jocasta agrees with me about the dangers of the cordless. Together we survey the great tangled mess of phone line now crisscrossing the hall. 'Hopefully,' Jocasta says, 'visitors will just think we're eccentric.' Not so our children, who have formed the view that we are clinically insane. I shout at the Space Cadet telling him to get off the mobile and use the landline. I even grab the phone and instruct his girlfriend that she, too, should be using a landline.

At this point, the Space Cadet looks as if a slow and agonising death from cancer might be preferable to life with his father.

Besides which, the landline is busy. Jocasta is using it, walking around the lounge room, dragging the phone and its ball of cord. She's involved in one of her favourite activities, talking to Batboy about his life at university. But Batboy's on his mobile and with every minute of pleasant discourse Jocasta can see the cancer cluster forming. With every second her desire to talk to her son does battle with her desire to protect him. And so she has him lie down on his bed with the mobile on loudspeaker, propped up on a pillow a good half-metre from his ear.

'What do you want?' Batboy shouts over the ravine that separates him from his phone. 'Shall I get a lead suit to wear whenever you call? Or keep the mobile in a little lead-lined trolley, which I could cart behind me wherever I go.'

Jocasta says she's willing to buy him just such a trolley, until Batboy reminds her about the dangers of lead.

It's not that I'm a Luddite (although I do have a strange aversion to looms); I just wonder why we are so unguarded and trusting when it comes to the new. If it's new, why is it always assumed to be better?

I like to play the trick of imagining that inventions occurred in reverse order. Imagine we only had 3-D films – a format so expensive that only mainstream movies can ever be made, with seen-it-all-before plots and action themes. Even worse, everyone has to wear those Buddy Holly glasses that get all sweaty and itchy after about five minutes.

Then, voila, someone develops 2-D movies. Suddenly films can be made for a fraction of the cost; there's a flowering of smaller, more eclectic works. Ticket prices drop. Even better, it's suddenly possible to kiss and make out in the back row of the cinema without your glasses getting tangled. Oh, thank you 2-D! What a revolution in filmmaking and viewing. What progress.

Or how about, after years of podcasting, someone invented this thing called AM radio. It's live, therefore right up to date, you can receive it on a device costing a few dollars and you can even interact with it, adding your voice to the debate, using a technique called 'talkback'. Oh, be still, my beating heart at this level of technical wizardry.

Then, to cap it off, someone could invent the very latest in telephony: a fixed-line phone. Superior sound quality. No batteries. An excuse to sit down for a moment.

Best of all: no cancer.

It's hard to calibrate anxiety levels when there are so many things to worry about. Too much anxiety and you'll tip into insanity; but without any anxious scepticism you fall victim to faceless corporations who really are taking liberties with your health.

Each week brings a new scare. The latest is about lipstick: it reveals that lipstick contains high levels of lead and that women consume 1.8 tonnes of the stuff over a lifetime, leading to everything from diabetes to stroke. From now on, I'm only going to kiss Jocasta through sheets of cling wrap. I'm fairly sure this places me in the category of 'totally insane'. I'm also convinced this is due to lead exposure through kissing.

A Philip Roth novel comes to mind, one in which the father's anxiety levels about his son's health are such that the son is forced to leave home. This kickstarts a series of terrible events in which all the father's worst nightmares come true and the boy is conscripted to fight in Korea, with the obvious outcome. If the father hadn't worried so much in the first place ...

Maybe I should calm down. Or focus my anxieties more narrowly. I weigh up the cordless phone against the kissing and decide Roth's probably right. I'll spend the next ten years of my life lugging around a huge tangled ball of phone cord, saving myself from cancer, only to trip over the wire and die suddenly from a cerebral haemorrhage.

I just hope Jocasta will kiss me as I go.

Pitch Imperfect

In its new advertising campaign, Woolworths reveals that the company's staff members are 'obsessed' with fresh fruit and vegetables. I don't know if this is a good thing. I'd be happy for my local manager to 'take a keen interest in …' or perhaps even 'spend some of his leisure hours thinking about …', but the word 'obsession' suggests a relationship to the world of cucumber, soft fruit and bagged lettuce that is, frankly, unhealthy.

'I'm totally obsessed,' I imagine him shouting as he throws himself on to the newly arrived pallets, his eyes ablaze like Gollum in *Lord of the Rings*. 'My precious, my precious,' he'll say as he fingers a particularly ripe rockmelon.

This sales pitch is hardly new. For some time Australia's retailers have employed their advertising dollars to suggest they are affected by some form of mental illness. From Mad Barry to Silly Solly, the industry has been home to those who wish to make a public confession of their own frothing insanity.

Most notable is the Crazy family, which appears to consist of two brothers locked in a battle to the retailing death – Crazy Clint and Crazy Clark. Clint has retail beachheads in Albury, Cessnock and Gosford. Clark is happily ensconced in Armidale, Ballina and Blacktown. One can only imagine the situation growing up in the Crazy family, and the horrors that led to this dreadful family rift. Does Crazy Clark recount some of his brother's childhood escapades and say: 'That Clint, you know he really was craaazzzzy.'

And what of the rest of the family? Are there no sisters with an interest in retailing? Crazy Cate, perhaps. Or Totally Insane Susan?

In truth, customers don't require stores to be run by people who are suffering from mental illness expressed via unsustainable discounting. We'd be happy if retailers merely pledged to have a reasonable shot at things. An advertising slogan that said, 'We're moderately competent players within the world of retailing' would at least have the ring of truth.

Why not indulge in full disclosure? 'Here at Colesworth we use our vast market power to crush farmers and squeeze workers, thus allowing us to offer prices that are not too bad, considering you get a free car park and a complimentary go with our trolley. The meat isn't as good as at your local butcher, the fruit and veg has been rendered tasteless by cold storage, then again do you really have time for local shopping, what with three kids to take to soccer, a dog with worms, and a back toilet with a busted ballcock? So please come in and enjoy what can only be described as our moderately acceptable service.'

Now that's an ad that people would believe.

Instead, it's all Crazy this and Mad that, alongside slogans that suggest a mania for a particular product line: 'Here at Roger's Stools, stools are all we think about.'

If true, that's a cry for help.

Or there's the Persian rug shopkeepers who, year after year, must humiliate themselves with a closing-down sale at ridiculous prices because once again their manager has foolishly over-bought on his latest trip to the Middle East. Why do they keep employing him? Is he smoking hashish on his buying trips?

The old ads for Mad Barry's portrayed a man so delusional he was unable to set prices capable of yielding a profit. Much like the purveyors of Persian rugs, Barry's insanity expressed itself through the over-ordering of stock, so vast truckloads had to be sold at a crippling loss. How this fool was put in charge of a major retail chain remains a mystery.

How will Coles respond to Woolworths' new campaign? Such is the competition between the two, whatever one does, the other must copy. You have cheap milk; then we'll have cheap milk. You have a self-serve checkout system of rage-inducing complexity; then we'll have a self-serve checkout system of rage-inducing complexity.

Coles must be fretting over the depiction of Woolworths staff as suffering an obsessive compulsive disorder, featuring an overly intense relationship with fresh fruit. The logic of the market insists that Coles goes one better: 'Most of our seafood-section staff suffers from clinical melancholia, our banana buyer has quite a drinking problem, and Trevor on the loading dock has just been arrested for exhibitionism.'

Or they could just tell the truth: 'Coles – it's the same as Woolworths, but hopefully our store is closer to your house.'

All Women are Beautiful

'You do realise that you are absolutely gorgeous.' I said this to a friend after listening to her moan about her appearance. She didn't miss a beat: 'Well, maybe if I lost just six more kilos.' She is obsessed with dieting, despite the way her current diet has left her so hungry that if someone mentions the word 'muffin' or 'biscuit' or even 'apple' in her presence, she goes all dreamy and repeats the word in the manner of a Buddhist monk. 'Muffinnn ... muffinnn ... muffinnn.' Really she should be on three diets: that way she might get enough to eat.

'You don't need to lose weight,' I said, vainly trying to jog her out of the deep trance into which she had tumbled.

'You are so wrong,' she said urgently. 'I need to lose heaps. I need to see if my old body still exists under all *this.*'

The word 'this' was accompanied by a hand gesture so florid, so theatrical, so full of self-contempt that it would only make sense if the lower half of her body had been replaced with that of Jabba the Hutt.

I sighed. Maybe I needed to widen my line of attack. 'You do realise that all men find all women attractive? You all spend so much time worrying about it, but men don't notice. We just see you, all of you, and think, "How gorgeous are they?" We are wonderfully, gloriously indiscriminate.'

'Well, thanks,' she said with an offended sniff, leaving me wondering whether indiscriminate appreciation was as sought-after a commodity as I had supposed.

A couple of years back I was asked to do a piece for a glossy magazine, in tandem with a female writer. I'd write a piece on 'what men really think about women' and she'd do a piece of similar length on 'what women really think about men'.

I filed my 800 words and the (female) editor loved them. I explained how men liked solving problems but weren't so good at merely sympathising with their partner's bad experiences; how we'd do anything for a laugh; and how we could have genuinely intense relationships with our male friends without it always involving a lot of talking.

So far so good. There was, however, she said, one problem. The first paragraph of my piece had to be cut. It was so unlikely as to be ridiculous. Her readers just wouldn't accept it.

That paragraph began:

Strange, but true: all men, straight and gay, think all women are beautiful. Okay, maybe not all. But nearly all. This is one thing we've got going for us: we are not judgmental; our aesthetic is eclectic.

'It's a nice thought,' she said, 'but men don't really think that way. They judge us all the time. You'll just have to start the piece some other way.'

I argued back, assured her of my seriousness and – grudgingly – she printed the piece as written.

Another time, I wrote a similar piece and this time posted a link on Facebook. I threw 800 words at the topic, perhaps hoping that mere length would prove my sincerity. Again the reaction was intense. Men liked the article and agreed it was pretty accurate. One young man drew me aside: 'I showed that piece to my girlfriend and said to her, "See, this is what I'm always telling you. Read what it says, it's exactly right."'

That was typical of the male reaction. They'd all had the experience of seeing their girlfriend parade around in a beautiful dress before saying, 'I can't wear this because it shows off my fat arms.' They were left thinking, 'What fat arms? I didn't notice fat arms. I just saw a beautiful woman in a beautiful dress.'

The female reaction? That was much more varied. Some women said, 'It's great to know this'; but lots of others had the same doubts as that female editor of the glossy magazine.

Among the comments:

- *Do you think he means it?*
- *I love this article; however, the writer is in a real minority.*

And this from a younger woman:

- *Such a phenomenally poignant article, but as a young person I fear that your attitude is one that guys my age would be very unfamiliar with.*

Maybe that young woman was right, but I doubt it. I have faith that young men today are just like other men. We see a female – one of an appropriate age – and most of the time think, 'Now there's a good looking woman!'

What a relief it would be if women could see themselves through men's eyes. Gone would be the 'puffy ankles', the 'fat arms in this dress', the 'really gross way this shirt gapes'. All of it gone. If only they knew: we don't even notice; we are oblivious.

A woman shimmers into view and suddenly a heavenly choir begins to sing. The whole weight of evolution bears down on us, the history of the planet itself. Our DNA thrums with one question: 'Could this be the opportunity I have long sought to fulfil my genetic destiny and to go forth and multiply, albeit in the nicest, consensual, mutually pleasurable way?'

Imagine a set of scales. All human history sits on one side: the whole development of the species, from single-celled organisms to more complex beings; the slow clamber onto land with the attendant struggle to turn gills into lungs, rather an effort, if you remember; the development of the opposable thumb; the struggle to walk upright ...

All of that, as I say, sits on one side of the scales. And a single pair of supposedly puffy female ankles on the other. Perhaps it's now clear that the battle is an unequal one.

The male gaze is largely a forgiving one – even when it is directed at the man's own body. A woman, perfect in almost every way, will stand before a mirror, her eyes searching out the one imperfection, the rest of her body dissolving as the imperfection grows to overtake the whole mirror. In the same way, the man, standing before the mirror, finds that his eyes also keep searching. They register the fact that some parts of the package may require work. But then they move on; they swivel, they search, they duck and weave, until finally they stumble across something good. It may be a single good bit – a flash of chest; a broadness of shoulder; a greying temple, surely the sign of intelligence – but by God it attracts his attention.

It is with this same optimistic gaze we assess our female acquaintances. It is not sexist. We merely offer to others the same level of sympathy, consolation and selective blindness that we offer to ourselves.

Speaking of which, have I ever shown you my rather shapely legs?

Better still, we know that the proper use of a gaze is to look boldly outwards and not too intently inwards. John Ruskin, the great Victorian aesthete, argued that it is better to be born in a slum, able to see the grand castle though the window, than to be born in the castle, only to spend a lifetime viewing the slum.

This, I think, is how we should all look at our own bodies. Certainly, the place needs repair, the drainage is dodgy and the foundations are sinking, but at least the eyes still work. As Ruskin implies, maybe it is better to be surrounded by beauty than to possess it yourself. Who would want to be beautiful if the cost were to be blind to the beauty of others?

I turn to my beautiful friend. 'Tea?' I ask her.

'Yes,' she says after a tiny struggle with herself. 'And half a muffin, if you have one spare.'

Ah, sweet victory. I think I may be finally getting through.

Shedding Responsibility

Is there anything more annoying than being lectured by your son on a topic about which you have long lectured him? Here's the Space Cadet last Sunday on the subject of our shed: 'The shed is a real mess. You can't find a chisel when you need one.'

Oh, really. Now why would that be?

Five years ago the chisel was right there, on the chisel shelf, between the other chisels, displayed in order of blade width. The workbench gleamed with a light coating of teak oil, a single hammer resting idly on its surface, ready for use. A sequence of saws rose against the wall much like the pipes of a church organ. A sheaf of sandpaper nestled in the second drawer.

The shed was perfect, mainly because my own incompetence as a handyman meant the place was hardly used.

Into this Garden of Eden marched the Space Cadet. At age fourteen he developed an interest in building things. It was a misfortune from which the shed has never recovered. With each project, the devastation was worse. He was an earthquake. He was a flood. He was the Roman army marching on Carthage, leaving the fields salted and crops burnt.

At the end of each project I'd instruct him to clean up, but somehow it never happened. I'd be forced to enter the devastated region to try to reassert order. The chisels would be liberated from beneath piles of sawdust and placed back on their shelf. The screwdrivers would be picked up off the floor – the floor! – and slotted back in their box. The nails, scattered on the bench, their jar having been upended – upended! – would be placed back in their container.

I didn't mind the first twenty or thirty times. It was good to see him having an interest. Then I realised the problem: every time the shed was clean, he'd instantly begin another project. A clean shed was an incitement to activity.

'Why didn't you make him clean up after himself?' I hear your question whistling by. I choose to ignore it. Sometimes one's parenting is imperfect, and such imperfection brings its own punishment. There is no need for the judge to award additional damages.

And so I tidy up after him. Yet, knowing that each tidy-up will bring forth a new project, the gap between tidying grows ever longer. Until slowly it extends to never.

That's where we are now. I'm on strike. I haven't cleaned up the shed since the beginning of the year. 'How bad could it get?' I asked myself. The answer was very bad. Soon it was difficult to get in the door.

By turning this way and that, stepping over toolboxes and squeezing past teetering piles of timber, you could occasionally come across an area of empty floor big enough to stand upon. From that vantage point, you could stare into the gloom and hope your eye might alight upon the tool that you wished to use. Not so much a needle in a haystack as an adjustable spanner in a solid cube of crap.

Surely at this point the Space Cadet would clean up the shed? Not quite. Instead, he moved his carpentry operation onto the outdoor wooden table, which in summers past had been the setting for barbecues, a few friends sitting around quaffing chardonnay and discussing the latest developments in the literary world, but which now features a bolted-on belt sander, a drop saw, a large pile of pine off-cuts and an old recycling crate full of tools going rusty.

I exaggerate, but only as to the elevated nature of the discussions once enjoyed around the now-destroyed table.

Jocasta says she wants the table back. She says the Space Cadet is like a colonising army seizing more and more territory, crushing the local populace until life itself loses all meaning.

I say, 'You're comparing your younger son to the Taliban?'

'Pretty much,' she answers, 'although without the oppressive mediaevalist ideology.'

Still I refuse to clean up the table. If we wait long enough the Space Cadet will be forced to act. Which brings us to last Sunday and his comment: 'The shed is a real mess. You can't find a chisel when you need one.'

I stare him down, expressing surprise at his surprise.

'I have plans,' he continues, 'to clean it out and set it up properly.'

'Good idea,' I say, as if the thought has stung me with its freshness and novelty.

So he removes everything from the shed and places it all on the back lawn – benches, shelves, piles of timber and bags of concrete. He repaints the interior and scrubs the floor. He installs new lighting. That was early in the week. Then it started raining.

The rain, I must say, didn't do a lot for the bags of concrete or for the sheets of chipboard. We now have a near-empty shed and a backyard that looks like New Orleans after Hurricane Katrina.

The wooden table, though, is free of tools – all of them given pride of place in the newly cleaned-out shed. It may be time to invite some friends over.

The Bin-it List –
Twenty-five Things to Avoid
Before You Die

The Bin-it List – Twenty-five Things to Avoid Before You Die

Everyone now seems to have a 'bucket list' – a record of all the things they want to do before they kick the bucket. So what about a 'bin-it list', comprising all the things you should avoid in the years between now and death? I'm working up mine right now.

Bungee jumping in New Zealand
Visiting the South Island of New Zealand is so dull that as early as the 1950s tourists began throwing themselves to their death merely to end the misery of their holiday. Concerned that passing sheep might be injured, local authorities insisted on tying ropes around the ankles of any visitor who ventured more than a few metres above sea level. The ropes, of course, didn't stop people throwing themselves off various high structures – their holidays were still terrible – but it did protect the sheep, since the person's fall would be broken a metre above the ground (the height of a fully grown sheep). All these

years on, the rope still works to minimise sheep deaths. The sudden deceleration experienced by the bungee-jumpers, however, is usually enough to blow out their retinas.

Which, at least, prevents any further sightseeing in New Zealand.

Crocodile spotting in the Northern Territory

Fierce, primitive and smelling of fish, the motel owners of Darwin will be pleased to accommodate you during your visit. They'll also be happy to arrange for you to be driven hundreds of kilometres to a foul mangrove swamp inhabited by crocodiles. Occasionally, you may see two eyes staring at you in a creepy fashion. This is just the captain's nephew Troy. He's quite harmless as long as the enclosure holds.

Downhill skiing

Some say the only people on the ski fields are rich folk from private schools who drive Porsches, but that's not true. There are also rich folk from private schools who drive Land Rovers. And rich folk from private schools who drive Audis. To join in, you'll need an array of specialist equipment: a credit card, a cash card, a wad of money, a cheque book and accidental death cover. Hand all these over at the ski shop and sign the insurance waiver, by which you agree that you are an insane person planning to hurl yourself off the top of a mountain with a slippery piece of wood tied to your feet. In return you will be given a ski jacket so puffy you will be unable to move your arms or legs, some goggles so scratched you'll be unable to see, and some boots so tight blood will spurt from your ears.

It's now time to decide which level ski run you wish to tackle. In Australia they are graded as to level of difficulty: the Beginner, the Intermediate or the Philip Nitschke. The trick is to gather enough speed to banish the memory of how much you spent in the hire shop ... so you'll want to choose the Nitschke. Once you reach 175 kilometres an hour, you may decide you wish to stop. Luckily skiing offers many techniques to achieve just this result, comprising (a) a full Christie; (b) a tree; or (c) a metal chairlift pylon.

Any of these methods will result in a chance to sample the superb, and expensive, medical facilities available at the bottom of the mountain.

All in all, skiing offers a real winter break. Usually of your left femur.

Driving across Europe

You jump into the hire car and stare at the unfamiliar controls as your whole family nervously chants: 'In Europe, they drive on the right.' The only way out of town is via a ring road on which locals stage a daily re-enactment of the chariot scene from *Ben Hur*, while you try to escape the carnage by changing lanes, indicating your intentions by activating your windscreen wipers.

Some days later, with only minor damage to the car, you emerge into a large, asphalted truck stop dotted with weeds and stretching towards the horizon. In Europe, this is known as the countryside and it's quite different from the cities. For example, it's a longer walk once the car breaks down.

Getting a Brazilian wax

It's true the map of Tasmania has, in the downstairs department, become a rarity; in most cases, it has been sculptured, plucked and clipped into a shadow of its former self. In most homes it's now more a case of 'Would you care for a quick gander at my South Stradbroke Island?'.

The question remains: is all this pain and expense necessary? Once you've got this far – both of you naked in a hot tub with Barry White on the iPod – do you really think your prospective partner is going to pause and say, 'Wow, your downstairs department is way too retro for me'?

And then there's the planning to consider: wax one night and you'll wane the next. The freshly depilated article is not designed for immediate use. That means an awful lot of forward thinking. You're essentially saying, 'I'm confident enough of achieving congress in the early hours of Sunday morning that I'm willing to fork out $75 bucks on Tuesday lunchtime to have the lot off and endure the accompanying indignities.' But what if your prospective date rings on Wednesday and cancels? You've prepared the landing strip and suddenly it's a no-fly zone.

Is the map of Tassie all that bad? Did it not offer its own attractions? And, best of all, did it not allow the moment to develop as it would – rather than the military-style planning required by the Brazilian?

Better, really, to rely on the heady aphrodisiac that is alcohol, desperation and the music of Barry White.

Going fishing

Give a man a fish and you'll feed him for a day, but teach him to fish ... well, teach him to fish and you'll leave him hungry for weeks, standing in the glare on some rickety South Coast wharf, slowly developing skin cancer as the kids chant, 'Can we go home now?' and his partner moans, 'Can't we go to Bali next time?', all the while feeding the fish with overpriced bait, the smell of which is so overpowering he doesn't even fancy catching one, not once he's seen how sad they look when, by some flukish chance, the melanoma-developer next to him manages to haul one in, all flapping and wriggling and struggling for breath.

No wonder vegetarianism starts to appeal – the proper non-fish sort of vegetarianism where you escape to some little cafe, with sweet breezes and hippy waitresses, and settle down to eat some cheese.

Golfing

Personally I've never played golf. I *like* my wife. For others though, golf represents the perfect opportunity to trudge around dressed as a clown while wheeling a large, weighted trolley. The aim is to complete the course in as few shots as possible, thus maximising your drinking time. Indeed, feel free to yell 'Four!' as you approach the clubhouse to indicate the number of rounds you intend to consume in your first five minutes at the bar.

Success at golf is entirely dependent on your swing, which will fall apart if (a) you think about it; or (b) you don't think about it. Best instead to strike the ball with as much force as you can muster, so that it dribbles forward in the manner you could have achieved by having a toddler blow on it. Just repeat this action sixty or seventy times and you may decide you like your partner more than you thought.

Having breakfast in bed

You sit there, folded in on yourself, a tray balanced precariously on your lap, trying to saw away at a sausage, every movement sending a tsunami of tea from cup to tray, while the one slice of toast sprays the sheets with crumbs, some of which will still be there days later, miraculously surviving countless brushings and flappings, and probably the nuclear holocaust. If breakfast in bed were the only thing humans knew, imagine the excitement when someone invented breakfast with a table and chair. You can picture people gushing in admiration. 'What, no more crumbs? No more spilt tea? No more trying to digest while simultaneously bending double as if in some sort of weird yoga pose?' The proud inventor would beam with pleasure. 'Yes – and we're planning to make a second chair, and perhaps even a third chair. That way it would be possible to dine with others.'

Why ignore 400 years of progress and dream of balancing hot food and drink on your lap?

Investing in a boat

Oh, they look fantastic when you are walking past. There's nothing like a large, shiny motor cruiser when viewed from the shore. You can just see yourself aboard: surrounded by a bevy of the rich and famous, all of them sipping chardonnay and badgering you for a go with your throttle.

Then you step aboard.

The deck lurches from side to side. The whole place stinks of engine oil. And the chardonnay is warm because the wind-driven fridge is on the fritz. At this point, the bevy of rich and famous start throwing up over the side. During the next four hours, everyone aboard will go through the two stages of seasickness. First you fear you are going to die; then you fear you won't.

This is why, on a beautiful weekend morning, all the boats are lined up in the marina, able to be admired by the passing pedestrian. The owners have been out on them. Once. Two decades ago. They are not about to repeat the experience. And so the boats all sit there, leaching money.

Motor cruisers achieve what socialists can only dream of: they determinedly and continuously separate rich men from their money.

Learning Latin

The old student rhyme had it about right:

Latin is a dead language
It is dead as dead can be

It killed Julius Caesar
And now it's killing me.

Purchasing a red convertible

The red convertible certainly looks great when observed by a married man from the driver's seat of his family hatchback, surrounded as he is by the detritus of family life, the windows smeared with dog slobber, the luggage compartment full of shopping, the baby seats circled by the strange, grey, furry stuff that only grows around baby capsules. Viewed from that particular perspective, the convertible looks pretty good as it glides past in the right-hand lane, an attractive woman in the passenger seat. Well, it looks good until you realise the guy bought the car just three days ago and only then as a last, vain attempt to cure his erectile dysfunction, itself a product of his failure at work and his loathsome marriage.

Understand also that the attractive woman's conversation is so wretched the man finds himself speeding up just to drown it out, at which point the car, driven too hard, will break down somewhere outside Bargo, in which place the couple will spend a miserable and cheerless weekend, climaxing – or, rather, not climaxing – in another misery-inducing episode of erectile dysfunction ...

Just as easy, really, to stick with the hatchback.

Purchasing technology in the week it is issued

It's so glamorous to be the first in your group to have the latest Apple product. Well, maybe it would be glamorous, except everyone else in the room is thinking, 'My God, he must have queued overnight in town, in the wind and rain, with all the other nerds. Doesn't he have anything better to do? Maybe he doesn't have a girlfriend. That's sad, isn't it, for a guy his age? I must try to be more friendly to him to help him better cope with what must be a crippling level of existential despair that expresses itself in the need to buy new gadgets.' That's what they're all thinking, but if you want to think it's glamorous ...

Renovating the house

Don't start. Wait until you are sixty-eight and get the professionals to do it. (See below: 'Working out your affairs ...'.)

Seeing your favourite singer live in concert

It's always some seventy-year-old rocker, and you're paying $300, plus dinner and a taxi both ways, in the hope of remembering your teenage years, except all the night reminds you of is how old he's looking and, by implication, how old you must be looking, so thank God he's so far away you can hardly see him and the sound's so crook you also can't hear him, especially seeing both you and he are deaf. For thirty bucks, you could have seen a young band from the front row ...

Skydiving

There are two ways in which you can test the existence of gravity. One is Isaac Newton's method of throwing an apple into the air and seeing if it comes back down again. The other is to hurl yourself from a fast-moving plane, some three kilometres above the earth's surface and see what happens. If you begin falling to earth at a sphincter-tightening rate of 240 kilometres an hour then, yes, gravity does exist and, yes, it is not your friend. Later you'll be able to answer other exciting questions, such as: will my parachute work? Why is the wind pushing me off course? And is that the Hume Highway just beneath me?

Staying in a remote Scottish hotel

An empty dining room with dim lighting and two tables set. Only three staff, one with a scar suggesting recent psychiatric surgery. An aggressive note on the back of the door, threatening to charge you 'at restaurant prices' should you even think about bringing food into your room. An off-putting bloodstain on the continental quilt cover. The faint smell of cabbage ...

Staying in an English hotel

After many wrong turns, you find the hotel you booked months ago, only to be greeted by a strange, dandruffy woman with bad breath who claims to have no record of your existence, right up to the moment you agree to pay double. The hotel is so depressing, you cry yourself to sleep, thus using up the three tissues left in the 'complimentary' tissue box, together with all the loo paper, neither of which will be replaced for the duration of your stay. Each time you complain, the strange, dandruffy woman shakes her head so vigorously that at least you feel you've had the promised white Christmas.

Taking a trip on a cruise liner

Okay, I haven't been on one, so maybe I'm missing something. Here's what I know: a thousand people you've never met, all plied with virtually free alcohol, and a floor that rocks from side to side until everyone chunders. Can it be just chance that they offer no means of escape?

Taking the scariest ride at the theme park

This involves paying large sums of money to sit on rides that 'look' dangerous mainly because they are, the engineering having been supervised by generations of toothless carnival workers whose main sources of income are the coins and wallets that fall into their hands when hapless members of the public are suspended overhead on the creaking and shuddering scaffolding erected by their homicidal great-great-grandfather. 'Ah, yes,' the fans say, 'but there's the adrenalin rush when you think you're about to die but then end up safe.' Yeah, fair enough, but you could have the same experience from a doctor who diagnosed you with lung cancer and then changed his mind seven minutes later – 'Paperwork error, my fault entirely.' He's not so popular, so why the enthusiasm for the Tower of Terror?

Visiting Indonesia

Indonesia has a rich and spiritual culture, if only you could hear anything over the sound of Tony and Trish from Woollahra bragging about how they bargained down their bechak driver from fifty cents to twenty cents and it only took them two hours of their holiday to do it.

Visiting Italy

Okay, you love the Italians but they don't love you back. They became bored with tourists in 1963. Demanding their affection, when they long ago moved on, is starting to look a bit stalkerish. Also, the coffee is better in Melbourne.

Watch purchasing

It would be great, finally, to have a really posh watch. Then, when you die, you could hand it over to the next generation, just like they say in all the advertisements for the Phenomenally Expensive Watch Company (company slogan: 'Last time Switzerland ripped off this many people there were stolen artworks involved').

All these Swiss watchmakers may produce excellent timepieces but are they accurate enough to measure how very slowly time goes once anyone buys one of their watches and begins to boast about it to their friends? In particular, how it can withstand pressure down to 300 metres under water – not that he's ever been SCUBA diving himself, but it's nice to feel one could go down 300 metres should one want to, besides which these things are bought for the next generation really, not so much a purchase as an heirloom, not that he has a child yet, or even a partner, young women tending to avoid him because he's so damned boring about this watch, you see, speaking of which ...

Watching more sport

Maybe it's just me, but could someone explain the point of watching sport? The outcome is entirely predictable.

One side will win. And, if not, the other side will win. People will run or, if it's golf, walk. Occasionally, the ball will be dropped into a hole or through a hoop or kicked or handled across a line and, depending on the sport, this will be considered either a good thing or a bad thing. One multi-millionaire will brag that he managed to get the ball past another multi-millionaire. At the end of the season, someone having won, they'll take a break and then start all over again.

Working out your affairs at an 'estate planning seminar'

Okay, you want to leave something to the kids – and organising it properly seems a good thing to do before you die – but surely giving the kids your cufflink box, Bob Dylan record collection, and your complete set of novelty egg cups will do the trick? Why attend a seminar when you could be busy spending your remaining cash so as not to burden your children with an inheritance large enough to ruin their character? Do the right thing. In the time you have left, ruin your own character.

Zestfully accepting middle age and making the most of it

Many people say we should 'grow old disgracefully'; that we should 'rage against the dying of the light'. They say growing older is all in your attitude, and they quote the perky American aphorism: *Dance like no one is watching, love like you'll never be hurt.*

This is terrible advice. I'd suggest an alternative: *Dance like your chiropractor is watching, love like you're sure to be caught.* Really, life just needs to be endured until you turn sixty-eight, at which point you can engage in the pleasurable project of exhausting the children's inheritance. (See above: 'Working out your affairs ...'.)

I could go on. Rollerblading. Sex with someone you don't know. Spa tubs. All, frankly, rubbish. At least so I'm told.

Ah, so few years left and so much to avoid.

Chapter 5

In which the Bible is
rewritten by IKEA,
Leibniz is put in his place
and some French women
remove all their clothing

King Rat

There's a mouse rooting around in the pantry cupboards. At least that's what I imagine it is. Late at night, when sound is amplified, it seems enormous. Not a mouse; a rat, at least. Or maybe a wombat. The sound gets louder. Perhaps Matt Preston is in there, peckish for a late-night snack.

Of all the ways in which I'm not a proper man, my dislike of rodents looms fairly large. Standing on a table shrieking would be my preferred response. I'm aware this is socially unacceptable. As a man, you are meant to be ready to deal with such matters.

'You there – do you have a penis?'

'Um, yes.'

'In that case, you'll need to handle the killing. Please enjoy.'

Personally, I'd rather bedeck myself with ribbons and sit like a princess, being served glasses of chilled pinot gris and refreshing snacks, and yet, because of this penis thing, I find myself forced to join the rodent jihad.

And so I head off to the hardware store to collect the weapons of war.

On the way, I think about my various run-ins with rats. The first was in high school when we had to dissect a rat in science. I can still see its little pink body pinned on the board, my scalpel gingerly pushing around its innards.

You'd think I'd be able to claim victory in this initial round. After all, the thing was dead and nailed onto a board and I was sixteen and as pretty as a foal.

Still it defeated me. After three prods at its tiny lungs, I turned green, felt woozy and fainted, lying splayed on the floor of the science lab, as immobile as the pinned-down rat, while my thirty-four classmates howled with laughter. The resulting months of jokes and comments remain my greatest contribution to the project of providing deep and abiding pleasure to others.

Then there was the compost nightmare of 2009, when I became aware that rodents were digging holes under the fence and using my compost heap much like a Sizzler salad bar. Every day, I'd apply a spade to the heap, sealing up their means of entrance, only to come back the next day to see fresh earthworks as they smuggled out supplies of food. It was like *The Great Escape*. They probably had faked identity papers and dog tags made out of cigarette tins. One of them, I'm guessing, looked like Steve McQueen.

I poured in enough poison to kill a horse, and at least one rat took the bait and thoughtfully died on the neighbour's side of the fence. The score now – Rats: 1; Me: 1.

And so we come to round three. At Hardware Hell, a range of devices is available – poisons, tiny mouse traps, even a device that promises to capture the mouse without you having to see the body.

I'm caught with indecision, until I spot it, there on the top shelf. It's a mouse trap so large it looks more like a mediaeval trebuchet. There's a massive spring and a deadly-looking hinged piece of metal. If you were planning to assassinate some minor European royal, this could do the trick. *Bang.* 'There goes the King of Spain.' *Reload.* 'Prince Charles is next.'

On the back of the packet, the manufacturers are keen to explain the excessive size of their product. 'Rodents in Australia are getting bigger,' they say. They don't mention global warming but that's the implication. Throw a few more tonnes of carbon into the atmosphere and we'll have rats the size of King Kong.

My eye glances down to the bottom of the device on which the brand name has been stamped into the metal. 'The E-rat-icator'.

Of course.

For a second I imagine the scene in the E-rat-icator factory when young Stephen from marketing runs up to the managing director's office and says, 'By God, I've got it. We should call the thing the "E-rat-icator".' A look of startled admiration creeps across the boss's face as he considers the beauty, the brevity, the pure poetry of the name.

'Go and see Mr Myles in accounts,' he says simply, almost humbly. 'I think a substantial raise is in order.'

I get home and very gingerly place the E-rat-icator in the bottom of the pantry cupboard, arming it with half a spicy fruit-roll biscuit. With some difficulty, I pull back the loaded spring. I'm aware that one wrong move and I'll lose an arm.

That night I stand in the dark stillness of the kitchen, listening. There's rustling and thumping. The thing is so big, it probably beeps when it reverses.

Suddenly, with a bang, the trap flies shut. I wait a moment then gingerly open the cupboard door. There's a tiny, tiny mouse, dead in this massive trap.

I feel terrible.

There are moments when being a man is not all it's cracked up to be.

The Bible According to IKEA

Home decorating is the new religion: it's often done on a Sunday, involves a visit to a large building (sometimes called Bunnings) and entails a generous donation being placed in the collection plate (or cash register). Then it's back home to install the shelves/light fittings/ballcock, at which point the words 'Jesus Christ' are often used.

Later, when the job is complete and displayed to others, a further devotional outburst can often be heard from the local congregation, such as: 'Oh my God. Sweet Jesus, what have you done?'

In this context, it's hardly surprising the IKEA catalogue has now overtaken the Bible as the book which has the most copies printed each year. Some see this as a sign of crisis – the ultimate triumph of materialism over religion – but that's to ignore the spiritual lesson embedded in the IKEA catalogue.

The store itself is a metaphor for life. You enter IKEA full of uncertainty, confused about which direction to take, before finding yourself swept along with the crowd. Despite all the twists and turns, it's almost impossible to choose your own path. It's also difficult to know when the end will come. Suddenly, you turn the corner and there it is: the end. As with life, you realise it's all over and you haven't really got what you came for.

Along the way, there are some good experiences, most notably the meatballs. (Scholars who have studied the ancient IKEA scripts explain that in this context the word 'meatball' is a metaphor for all the earthly pleasures, such as sex, rock 'n' roll and watching reality TV while drunk.)

Meanwhile, IKEA's furniture is like a biblical text. Its ability to fall apart within a few years reminds us of the impermanent nature of existence. The way the shelves bend when overloaded indicates the dangers of focusing too much on collecting worldly possessions. And the use of veneers glued onto a cheap chipboard structure is surely a lesson about valuing what is real and deep.

Certainly the Bible teaches us about the treacherous nature of the surface of things ... and so does a Billy bookshelf left out in the rain.

Putting together your piece of furniture brings further insights. Success is born of patience, diligence and an understanding that there will always be a mystery to existence: in this case, the one bolt that's always left over.

Given the rich spirituality of IKEA, the church now has little option but to ditch the Bible and start basing its lessons on what is the more popular book. You can imagine the priest standing atop his flat-pack pulpit, the Allen bolts glinting amid the chipboard: 'Today's lesson is taken from the IKEA catalogue 2013, pages 10 and 11, the erection of the Lillangen.'

There will be a shuffling sound as the congregation turns to the correct page.

And, verily, did the man become sorely distracted, for he hath confused the plugs marked A with the plugs marked B, and when the plugs marked B did not fit in the holes marked A, he did become full of a terrible wrath and, lo, did he smite those plugs marked B with his hammer, aka 'the home handyman's screwdriver', thus breaking them and making the whole Lillangen impossible to assemble. And, verily, did his wife look at the shattered mess and say unto him: 'Next time we'll have to get a proper bloke in.'

And the man, who was sorely tired, replied, 'Do not forsake me in my time of need, for I am greatly ashamed.'

Verily, did he then show his wife the assembly instructions and how they contained no words, but markings only: strange runes, as one might find on an ancient temple, with hatched bits, and eyeballs, and things circled, and arrows flying here and there as if it were the Battle of Agincourt.

'And so verily,' the man sayeth, 'did I smite the plug marked B with my hammer, so great was my confusion and my sorrow.'

And, at that, the woman did forgive him, for not only is forgiveness divine but it's also fair enough, once you've had a squiz at the completely baffling instructions.

Of course, once you let one piece of IKEA furniture into your home, it does tend to multiply. As the priest will no doubt note:

And the Billy begat the Hemnes, and the Hemnes begat the Samtid, and the Samtid begat the Torsby.

'Shop once at IKEA,' the priest will say, a cheeky smile playing on his lips, 'and a month later it's like living with the band members of ABBA – your bum in a Bjorn and your feet on a collapsible Frida.'

And the parishioners will laugh at that one because it's true.

Both priest and congregation will then close their catalogues and raise their voices in song. 'All things cheap and portable, IKEA makes them all.'

And a good thing they do. Especially once you consider the spiritual guidance that lies therein.

A Misery of Spinach

Why do high-end chefs hate food so much? They're always forming it into discs, exploding it into foam or placing it in high-rise stacks. A few weeks ago, on a rare excursion to an upmarket noshery, I ordered the flathead, expecting, well, flathead. Suburban of me, I know.

A long plate arrived on which discs of the thoroughly defeated fish were strung like coins flung towards a beggar. A dark sauce had then been drizzled over the lot, much in the way that a gangland killer might splash kerosene over his dying victim. The dish should have been called 'a revenge of flathead'.

Today's chefs seem particularly worried that someone might recognise the type of protein that's been used in a dish. The phrase 'my chicken looks like chicken' would cause heartbreak in most city kitchens. It's as if they are running a witness protection program for food. The chicken is disguised as a city apartment block, while the lamb chops lurk nearby pretending to be shrubbery.

These transformations may be exciting for the restaurateurs of the moment, but a word of caution is required from those of us who lived through the 1970s. Ladies and gentlemen, we have been down this road before. The chefs of today are blithely heading towards the horror that is fish in a mould.

The 1970s were a decade in which white sauce, optimistically named 'béchamel', was poured over everything, no doubt in an attempt to glue together the vegetables, all of which had been boiled to a point three seconds shy of disintegration. My mother really only had one dish. It was confidently titled 'tuna mornay' and involved a can of tuna being assaulted with what appeared to be a bucket of wallpaper paste. It could either be eaten or saved for later use as a school craft project.

My father's cooking involved 'Welsh rarebit', his optimistic name for cheese on toast, and 'eggnog', his optimistic name for a raw egg stirred into a glass of milk. When he was cooking I'd be so starved of vegetables I'd have an urge to graze on roadside verges. He also had a tendency to burn things, so that dinnertime often involved a visit from the fire brigade. By the time I was fifteen I was like Pavlov's dog, salivating whenever I heard a fire siren.

My father was not alone in this approach. There was a view that if you were going to cook something, you should really cook it. When barbecuing, the aim was to defeat that T-bone steak and show it who was boss. Cooked right, it would emerge with the outside blackened and the inside grey – perfectly matching the boiled-to-death brussels sprouts with which it was served.

By the late 1970s, you could accurately measure your distance from Sydney by the reaction you'd get when asking for a steak cooked 'rare'. In Darlinghurst they'd nod and hop to; in Bathurst, they'd query the order and finally agree; and in Broken Hill, the cook would come out of the kitchen for a good long stare.

There were rules about cooking; they were just different from today's rules. Nearly every dish, it was generally agreed, could be improved by the addition of canned pineapple. A bird called the chicken and a fruit called the apricot were considered natural allies. And when the occasion was fancy, the best way to serve the fish was in a mould.

Here's the secret – and I know it's going to appeal to today's young chefs – you take a fish that is shaped like a fish. You then pulverise the bastard and pour in about three horses' worth of gelatine. (There was no need to boil down your own horse; even in the '70s we had gelatine in a packet.) Next, you pour the fish and gelatine mix into a fish mould, whereupon it ends up looking identical to the fish with which you started. Identical except it tastes rubbish and involved four hours' work.

And this is aside from the trend towards 'deconstructed' food, in which you take an old recipe and 'deconstruct it' by placing all the ingredients separately on a plate. Thus, a 'deconstructed peach melba' has a serving platter on which sits a peach, a blob of ice-cream and a puddle of raspberry sauce. Patrons then 'reconstruct' the meal by blending the materials with their spoon.

This has to be the best labour-saving idea since the invention of the cotton loom. Presumably, the chef is out the back smoking Gauloises and doing the crossword, freed from the necessity of actual cooking.

Once these trends start, it's hard to know where they'll stop. Why go to the trouble of putting the ingredients on a plate? Why not just give patrons the keys to the kitchen and suggest they root around in the fridge? Or sit all your customers in a row and pelt them with fresh ingredients. 'Here's your prawn cocktail,' says the waiter, lobbing in a lettuce, a bag of prawns and a tub of cream.

The patrons would fall upon the food like hungry dogs, the flavours mingling in the resultant mêlée.

The cutting-edge restaurant could try more complex recipes. A cold blended soup – gazpacho comes to mind – would see each customer handed a tomato, a cucumber and a capsicum. They would chew them thoroughly, then, with the ingredients stored in their mouths, join hands to perform a Mexican folk dance, thus replicating the work of the blender. Only when properly mixed would the chef remove the cigarette from his mouth and invite the guests to swallow.

Amid all these trends, I just wish there was room for more honesty. Instead of 'a ballotine of salmon with cucumber and tarragon dressing', I'd like to see dishes such as 'a disappointment of fish' or 'an affront of chicken' or 'a how-dare-you of quail' – served with 'a misery of spinach'. The names would better reflect the feeling of 'Oh, didn't I order badly!' that inevitably accompanies a night out at any of the best restaurants.

The Miracle in Mexico

I'm sitting atop the Pyramid of the Sun at Teotihuacan in Mexico, considered by some the most spiritually powerful place on the planet. Three young French women, standing five or six metres away from me, have just removed all their clothes. They throw their arms skywards and wiggle their pale white bottoms in my direction. The sun comes out from behind some clouds to illuminate the scene more clearly. The temple has more power than I thought.

I imagine they are on a mutual dare. It's taken them a few seconds to pull off their tops, pull down their skirts and salute the sun. Their young male friend, sitting to my side, clicks off some photos; they then rapidly slip back into their clothes, smoothing down skirts and tops. A minute later, it's as if nothing has happened.

Maybe nothing has. Is this another manifestation of the slow-motion accident called 'being a middle-aged man'? Maybe I have finally cracked and have taken to imagining young women removing their clothing atop sites of historical significance when they're just admiring the view? Maybe if I clambered up the Empire State Building or caught a lift to the top of the Eiffel Tower I could enjoy similarly debauched delusions.

I'm relieved to note that Jocasta is also looking in their direction. So is our tour guide, a devastatingly handsome young Mexican who, earlier, had described his own good looks by reference to the DVD region code for his country.

'I am,' he'd stated with quiet confidence, 'a zone-4 Johnny Depp.'

Right now, he swivels towards me, his lush Johnny Depp ringlets bobbing with glee.

'Did you see that?' he asks. I nod and wistfully he looks back at the French girls.

'I just wish it was my day off.'

He shakes his head in disbelief at the tragedy of his situation. As a zone-4 Johnny Depp, the only barrier between him and twenty-four hours of glorious rumpy-pumpy in a motel with three French women is, it appears, his own lack of immediate availability.

As for myself, I don't think they'd be keen. For a start, there's the matter of my own looks, those of an Australian-zone John Goodman, and my left knee, which has seized up in recent months, giving me the gait of a broken-down horse on its way to the knackery.

Even Jocasta, who claims to appreciate my other virtues, is less than impressed by the knee. In the weeks leading up to our trip to Mexico, she'd made her views clear: 'We're going on hikes, long ones, up and down mountains and into isolated towns. I don't want to hear a lot of moaning about the knee.'

I'm keen to be the outdoor adventurer she wants me to be. In the week before we left, I'd commenced an intensive course of fish oil, glugged straight from the bottle, and shark cartilage tablets, taken at a rate of five times the recommended dose. Both were advertised as the solution to a seized-up knee. By the time we clambered onto the plane I smelt like an Arctic cannery and the theme to *Jaws* played whenever I moved.

Back at the Teotihuacan temple, I sit with my bad leg stretched out, pushing it down into contact with the ancient stones. Before the French girls distracted me, I'd been trying to imagine the cosmic rays entering my knee and doing their good work.

Behind me, a group of American Christians have long settled into a circle. Dressed in white, with their arms looped together, they are chanting Bible passages in what sound like the smooth accents of Minnesota. So involved are they in their religious experience they are oblivious to the temple-top striptease.

The French girls, meanwhile, are chatting to their friend, giggling over their achievement. Zone-4 Johnny can't take his eyes off them. Perhaps he could just dump his tour group – us – and announce to the girls his willingness to play.

The French women wander over – and head for me. They hand me their camera. In hesitant English, one of them asks, 'Could you, please?'

Zone-4 Johnny looks aghast. 'Why him?' he's thinking.

We go back to the spot at which they removed their clothes and they pose for another picture, now including their male friend.

The clothes, alas, stay on.

We chat for a while and then Zone-4 Johnny indicates that our trip is over. We start the long climb down the 248 steps of the Pyramid of the Sun. I trot behind him and suddenly realise: my knee no longer hurts.

Hallelujah. I've been cured.

But how? Was it the chanting Minnesotans channelling the power of a Christian God? Was it the mystical and ancient power of the pyramid? Or just the sudden exposure to naked women?

A cure this miraculous needs further investigation. Each possible effect must be tested, and tested again, together with detailed exploration of any questions that may emerge. For example: Do the naked women have to be French? Would three representatives of the Czech Republic have a similarly medicinal impact? If the number of naked women were doubled would the effect be twice as powerful?

The road of science is a long and arduous one, but I shoulder my burden. Already, my left knee tingles in anticipation of the arduous study that lies ahead.

Fair Go, Leibniz

Leibniz, they say, was the last human to know everything; what a shame I'm the first human to have forgotten everything. Leibniz lived at a time when knowledge was limited; he studied and memorised all that was available. I live at a time of endless knowledge, much of which has been poured into one ear and leaked out the other side. Whole periods of school have left a single fact looming like an unstable chimney on an earthquake-devastated plain.

Kindergarten to Year 3: *i* before *e* except after *c*. I scrunch my forehead and try to remember more but that's it. Four years and one rule which doesn't even work most of the time – at least not like a rule of *science*.

Years 4 to 6: Wentworth, Lawson and Blaxland discovered the way over the Blue Mountains. Years 7, 8 and 9: No they didn't. Indigenous Australians already knew.

That's another six years gone, the second three years cancelling the first three. Year 10 is a blank. In year 11, Mao went on a long march but I can't remember why. Year 12 involved Hamlet but the exam question was about the ghost and not the young prince and how unfair is that? The play will forever be coloured by feelings of bitterness and remorse.

In geography all we did were interminable lessons on the formation of oxbow lakes. The panel of three diagrams – the first showing a river with a slight bend, the second showing a bigger bend, the third showing the lake detaching like a tear-drop – were repeated so often that most Australians of my generation could accurately reproduce them while blindfolded and under threat of execution.

There was wisdom, of course, in this method. By requiring students to repeat the same diagram over twelve years of schooling, one was given a sense of geological principles: in particular, the sensation of being worn down over time.

Through a combination of budgetary caution and blind loyalty to the Mother Country, most Australian schools were kitted out with maps from the 1940s, in which India and most of Africa were painted pink to indicate British rule. Years later, I find myself searching newspapers in vain for the latest news from Abyssinia, Ceylon and Mesopotamia. I'm also keen to take a holiday in Siam but can't find the brochure at Flight Centre.

Leibniz had it lucky. In his time, there was so little to know. Not for Leibniz, the sensation I have each time I pass by the newsagency and try to decode the poster for *Who* or *New Idea*: 'Inside Tori and Brad's wedding';

'Fresh fears for Simone and Rob's baby'; 'Laura and Tom eat lunch'.

Who are these people? Am I the only one baffled as to their identity? Would it kill them to include a surname or two for those of us who are a bit slow on the uptake?

In Leibniz's day there was an agreed canon of knowledge. Diderot summarised the lot in his *Encyclopédie*. Over a series of volumes, he listed all you needed to know. I'd like someone to attempt a new version:

- Brad Pitt and Angelina Jolie are actors. They live together and have children, some of whom are adopted.
- There's a particle accelerator near Geneva where they have discovered the 'God particle'. (If anyone asks for further details, fall to the ground and pretend there's a chicken wing caught in your throat.)
- It was a mistake for the Greeks to enter the eurozone.

The problem is we all know different things; we then assume everyone should know the bits that we know. Listening to the evening quiz on the radio, I snort with derision at the person who cannot name King Lear's three daughters but then sigh at the science question that follows: 'What is the chemical symbol for water?'

How dare the ABC ask something so ludicrously difficult on what is meant to be a popular quiz?

Before I listen again, I'll need to memorise more of the agreed knowledge of our times:

- Adele is a British soul singer who has sold an enormous number of records and has a decent voice.
- Einstein was terribly smart and worked out how time and space work.
- Bernard Tomic is a tennis player and not a golfer.

In the absence of such a volume, I am left to the taunts of the young. I wave them away, like so many annoying flies. I tell them, 'I've forgotten more facts than you'll ever know.'

This, though, is my problem: there's no reward for having once known something.

I'd like to see that remedied with a TV quiz show in which you could win by offering the mere remnants of knowledge.

'Yes, the gold rush. It happened. It was definitely after 1788 and yet before Gallipoli.'

Correct!

'The Beatles had a drummer called Pete Sutcliffe but he left before they were successful.'

Pretty much there! Correct!

'In geography, a glacial lake is called a carn, torve, or maybe a tern. It's a short word, I know that, and it sounds like an IKEA storage unit.'

Near enough! Correct!!

Leibniz, I challenge you. All I need are the right rules and victory will be mine.

Great Diets of History

For months now I've been on the 5:2 diet – a punishing regime in which you half-starve yourself for two days a week, then eat normally for the other five. This mirrors a time in human history when people would kill a woolly mammoth, eat well for a few days, then starve while searching out their next meal.

The diet seems sensible – just model your eating on a period of history in which obesity was uncommon. Surely, though, there are other epochs for publishers to exploit.

The British Navy diet

Obesity was rare in the British Navy of the late 1700s, so what was it about the mighty square-riggers that kept people so thin? Sir Winston Churchill, some say, described the British Navy as having traditions of 'rum, sodomy and the lash', and all three are featured in this practical and easy-to-use diet. While the rum-drinking may be attempted solo, other aspects require a group approach.

The Ancient Egypt diet
The ancient Egyptians were known for their lean physiques, but only now is science unlocking their health tips. The secret, it seems, consists of being forced to drag giant stones across the desert, thence to install them in a pyramid, all while being whipped and fed modest amounts of unpalatable bread. The *Ancient Egypt Diet Workbook*(TM) contains an easy-to-use meal planner ('Buy small amounts of bread then eat them') and instructions for an authentic fourth-dynasty whip. (Building materials not included.)

The French Revolution diet
Sometimes known as the 'Madame Defarge weight loss program', this is the world's only diet guaranteed to eliminate three to four kilos in less than a second. All you have to do is oppose the current system of government and brace yourself. (Only available in jurisdictions which permit beheading.)

The English workhouse diet
If you've ever seen the musical *Oliver*, one thing is instantly apparent: the lead character is whip thin. How come? The secret, scientists now believe, lay in his diet. Oliver, without even knowing it, practised an extreme form of food restriction now linked with improved mood and increased longevity. A crucial hint comes early in the story, when young Oliver holds an empty plate to the manager of his accommodation/workplace situation and requests, 'More please.'

'This indicates he was suffering hunger,' says Professor Troy Umbrage, in a paper just published in *Proceedings of the American Society of Dieticians*. 'Once we understand that he was hungry – or "calorie restricted", as we now term it – it's hardly surprising he achieved a lean appearance and such a positive attitude to life.' Troy's book – *A New Twist on Dieting* – gives recipes for Oliver's diet (gruel, daily) and recommends his calorie-burning activities (workhouse labour, eighteen hours a day). 'Art contains many dietary tips,' says Troy. 'In *La Bohème*, Mimi's hand is described as frozen. That's partly the tuberculosis, of course, but I'd love to see a chart of her HDL/LDL cholesterol ratios. One serve of oily fish and that girl could have been saved.'

The Mao Zedong Long March diet
What a straightforward diet this is: simply walk 12,000 kilometres while being pursued by the Kuomintang. You'll marvel as the weight just falls off. During the Long March, Comrade Mao assisted those with 'diet jitters' by shooting them and leaving their corpses to rot 'like offal which floats to the surface of the ocean through which the people swim'. In today's version, a personal trainer will instead scream belittling comments from the sidelines.

The Alexander the Great diet
First conquer much of the known world. Then discover you don't like Indian food. There's nothing like marching 6,000 kilometres only to find you really don't care for

what they do with the fish. It tastes okay when you are eating it, but all those spices are a nightmare for the indigestion.

The pre-humanoid diet

Forget the caveman diet – our most common health problems began further back, in the period when we began to walk erect. Aching backs, tension headaches and really bad bunions: none of these existed before we came down from the trees. Was that moment a wrong turn for humanity? 'It's a possibility worth investigating,' says expert Barbara Tourniquet. Adherents of this diet spend their time swinging from tree to tree and eating bananas. Already there are signs of fewer bunions and less back pain (although some report inner-thigh chafing from the rough tree trunks).

The Devonian diet

It was during the late Devonian Period – about 375 million years ago – that our fish ancestors first developed the primitive breathing systems that allowed them to crawl on land for short periods. But should they have stayed put? Fast-food restaurants, industrialised food production, the consumption of sugary soft drinks – all would be impossible if our species were still water-based. With The Devonian diet, adherents eat nothing but pond scum, copying the obesity-free period before Tiktaalik Roseae so thoughtlessly tried to haul itself out of the water.

Or you could just eat less.

The Junk Yard

Is there a statute of limitations on all the stuff left in the family home once the children become adults? How long does it need to sit there, unclaimed, before it can be thrown out with a clear conscience? Many parents complain about running a hotel for their grown-up children; I'm more concerned we've become a branch of Kennards Self Storage.

There are presidential libraries in the US that have less detailed archives. Certainly, the defeat of the Burwood Titans by the Leichhardt Saints in the winter of 1998 was a moment of soccer history that will live on in the minds of those present, but do we really need three copies of the newsletter recording Batboy's heroic save just before the half-time whistle? Not to mention the soccer jersey in which the game was played?

And while I look forward to having grandchildren, is it really worth hanging on to three boxes of apple juice-stained Little Golden Books, many of which appear to have been chewed either by rodents or their original owners? Yet I dare not throw them out.

The last week of the holidays involved moving large quantities of junk from one place to another. The laundry drawers are now tidy but you can't open a single cupboard elsewhere in the house without being crushed by an avalanche of recently moved junk. Next summer, I will clean out the cupboards and carry all the rubbish out to the shed, enjoying the momentary delusion that this represents some sort of progress.

Tidying up, I now realise, is like the water cycle: stuff moves through the system without a molecule ever being lost. We now live perched on a midden of our own making, comprised of bicycles without front wheels, baseball mitts where the leather has gone all funny, and skateboards picked up in the council clean-up of 1999 and never ridden.

A reasonable person would say 'throw it all out', yet already I can hear the plaintive tone of the grown-up child, standing at the doorstep in ten or twenty years' time: 'I've come to pick up that bike. I've just come across a front wheel that would fit perfectly.'

And then the look of outrage when you make your confession: 'Threw it out twenty years ago, mate. Thought you didn't want it.'

'I left it on purpose,' they'd say, gripping the hand of the disappointed grandchild who had been promised the bike, a tear beginning to snake down her cheek. 'I left it with you for safekeeping.'

The word 'safe' would be emphasised as if the whole contract of parenting had been ripped up in this one treacherous act of bike disposal. Soon, the grandchild would be sobbing deeply, her tears only stanched by your promise to immediately purchase the bike of her choice at the nearest retailer.

Perhaps I feel the matter too keenly due to the crimes committed by my own father. I was twenty-three when I visited the family home to pick up my incomparable collection of Elvis LPs – a collection so broad, so loving of the King that it extended to proof-of-fandom purchases such as the only-quite-good soundtracks of *Harum Scarum*, *Speedway* and *Girls! Girls! Girls!*

I won't trouble you with a description of the rather shifty look that came across my father's face when I made my inquiry as to the collection's current storage point but will simply, in a dignified fashion, record my own response to his revelations: 'Noooo! Nooooooo!' (Falls prone on driveway, beating hands on ground and kicking feet.) 'Why? Why? Why me? My life is over. How could you do this to me?'

Showing his remorse by prodding at my body with his foot while taking a contemplative drag on his pipe, my father attempted the usual explanation. 'I thought you didn't want them.' Then he tried to brighten the mood by recording the enthusiasm of the woman at St Vincent de Paul, noting her chirpy response: 'We should be able to get heaps for all of these.'

Later, I asked for my collection of Biggles books (gone), the tiny battery-operated record player on which I used to play singles (gone) and my John Travolta-style white suit (also gone but on this my father perhaps had a point).

And so, three decades on, I move the bicycle-without-a-wheel from one location to another, the contraption providing considerable more exercise in the lifting than it ever did in the riding. With other items, my hands twitch, reaching towards the bin. The school reports (keep, of course). The baby health diary (keep, of course). And the geography homework for Year 10 (come on, it has got to go).

Then, in my mind, it is back to the doorstep and Batboy standing before me in twenty years' time: 'My son, Sebastian, is having trouble understanding the water cycle. I wonder if you could fish out my old essay on the topic. Surely you kept it …'

Maybe we could strike a deal: I'll keep all his crap if he can just find me a second-hand copy of *Girls! Girls! Girls!*

Chapter 6

In which a world record
is broken, a literary map
is drawn and the niceness
epidemic is revealed

Nice Try

Society becomes nastier by the day, according to a million newspaper articles, but the real scourge, surely, is the rise of competitive niceness. Consider the tussle over who'll pay after a visit to the coffee shop:

'I've already paid.'

'Well, I'm paying you back.'

'I don't want your money.'

'Here, I am putting it in your shirt pocket.'

'I'll just take it out and leave it here on the table, what happens to it then is your business ...'

All this over $3.10 for a soy latte.

Then there's the 'you first' 'no, you first' hand gestures between motorists squeezing through a chicane. Or the painful longueur at the lift as one person says, 'After you', then the other says, 'No, I insist', then the first smiles and says, 'Well, only because the rule is age before beauty'.

I suppose it's pleasant enough. But do we really have time for this sort of stuff in our thrusting modern economy?

Most workplaces are shared with about twenty people. In a day's work, wandering back and forth from the mailroom, you pass the same people again and again. Etiquette, however, insists upon a greeting each time, a whole orchestra of sounds, from the first trilled 'Good morning' at 8.30am, to the jokey 'Hello again' at 8.35am, to the somewhat tight-lipped 'Hi' at 8.40am, deteriorating into a series of strangulated squawks, a high-pitched 'argghh', followed by a low-pitched 'um', then a middle-pitched 'eh', as if you were collecting notes towards a jazz record.

Spotting each other on the bus chugging home, by all means treat yourself to a jaunty 'You again!' but can we leave it at that? When we first meet in the morning, can we consider ourselves familiarised for the full eight hours?

Meanwhile, the whole business of fetching the coffee has become a nightmare. It starts with an innocent 'I'm going for coffee, anyone else want one?' and ends with six people brandishing banknotes at each other, like the circle of guns in *Reservoir Dogs*, the voices climbing over each other in disputation, 'Let me', 'No, it's my turn', 'You bought them Tuesday', until victory, naturally, is achieved by the one who first offered to walk to the coffee shop.

She heads off, someone yells, 'Can you also get me a danish?', and the whole deal collapses, money now changing hands, proving that even niceness has its limits. (The limit right now: we'll shout $3.10 for a coffee, but no way $5.40 for the added danish.)

Of course, things worsen once you depart the office and enter the suburbs. There are neighbourhood barbecues that are now impossible to leave. The hosts certainly want everyone to go home, and the guests are more than ready to leave, it's just a matter of finding the words that allow this mutually yearned-for outcome to occur.

'We must make a move.'

'But you'll stay for one last drink, and perhaps a last slice of cake? It's Andrea's mother's recipe.'

'Well, it does look good.'

That's the start of a process still going at 3am, the weary hosts stumbling forward with yet more remnants of cake; the dishevelled guests spooning in another plateful of the now-repulsive confection, washed down with the warm chardonnay left at the bottom of the cheapest bottle.

'Really, we should think about ringing the cab.'

'But it would be a terrible waste to not finish it off.'

I wouldn't be surprised if, in the depths of East Hawthorn, or the Amish belt of North Wahroonga, there are dinner parties that commenced in 1972 and are still going strong, neither host nor guest wanting to be so rude as to call it quits. You might stumble in and find them all wearing their safari suits and muu-muus, prodding with a well-used Splade at their 8495th slice of pavlova, still wondering whether Gough Whitlam made it across the line in the December election.

'It might be time to leave,' one of the guests might finally mumble, realising it's been forty years. That's when the hosts will bring out their required lines:

'Just one more cup of coffee for the road.'

Or 'One last go in the pool, just to cool down.'

Or 'If you eat this last sausage, we can wash the platter.'

It's not only the old-money belts of Sydney and Melbourne. In other parts of the country, Greek, Italian or – worse – Iranian aunties may be involved. Warning: DO NOT ENTER THESE HOUSEHOLDS. Well, not unless you have acquired a medical certificate limiting the amount of food you may accept.

Even then, you'll get disputation. 'This medical certificate of yours ... I notice it doesn't explicitly mention baklava, and, really, baklava is a health food, it has no calories, it has nothing bad in it, and you've only had forty-seven slices so far, which is really unfair to my grandmother, whose recipe this is, and she always said it was the forty-eighth slice which was the best, so if you just hold still and open wide ...'

Really, it's no good fighting. We must square our shoulders, gird our loins and smile in the face of the niceness epidemic.

Perhaps I can begin by offering you another slice of cake?

Atlas Hugged

We're near Nowra, driving down the Princes Highway, when we see a sign to the right. It's for a town called Sassafras. There's something enticing, almost erotic, about the name itself, all those sibilants playing on your lips and tongue. I enjoy the feel of it, Sass-a-fras. It's a sylvan glade, I'm sure, with a creek bubbling through. Moss on one side, dappled sunlight on the other. There'll be a small pub, a shop run by a leather craftsman, and some houses nestled into the hills. We turn inland and head for our new destination, the place growing ever more wonderful in our minds. Sometime later, we turn a corner and there's a single road sign and a broken-down barn. That's Sassafras.

Australia is full of these towns that don't really exist. Out west, the landscape is dotted with them; a large bull's-eye on the map drawing you in. 'We'll stop there for petrol and a delicious counter meal,' you say to each other as you calculate the distance to this thriving settlement. An hour later you arrive. There's a road sign half-eaten by termites and a farm gate with an angry dog.

For all these disappointments, I'm still a big fan of maps. I can't imagine a holiday that doesn't start with a map – the intrepid voyagers standing at the kitchen table, the map spread out, letting themselves be tempted by a patch of national park, the curve of a beach, an intriguing place name.

Recently the death has been announced of the 'glove-box *Gregory's*' – the street directory that has guided drivers for seventy-five years. The publication has fallen foul of GPS technology – the insistent, slightly maddening voice that now directs our every move. I understand the attraction of the GPS navigator. You don't have to stop and look at the map. You are warned to change lanes. And you don't have to rely on your partner, who has spent the past forty minutes holding the map the wrong way up.

Marriages have been saved, collisions averted and petrol saved.

The price is that you can only ever arrive where you've already planned to go. The GPS is about setting a route and then following it. It turns the driver into a cog in the machine. There are times when it directs you the wrong way down a one-way street and you half-convince yourself it's not your responsibility. 'Don't blame me, officer, I was just carrying out orders.' In the battle between yourself as a sentient being and a cheap electronic device, the cheap electronic device just won.

More importantly, you never get to study the map, to be enticed by other possibilities. And you never get to see your progress across the map; to understand how the town you're heading for relates to the river on this side or the mountains on that.

Many of my favourite books start with a map. *Eastern Approaches* by the diplomat and adventurer Fitzroy Maclean has a beauty – a bit of old-fashioned cartography headed 'Central Asia', the mountain ranges stained in various shades of brown, the depth of waterways marked with contour lines, as if the sea were vibrating. It's impossible to look at it for a few moments and not daydream about being in Tashkent or Samarkand or Birsk.

Or there's the map in Laurie Lee's *As I Walked Out One Midsummer Morning*, showing the poet's progress across Spain in 1935 and 1936, walking and sleeping rough, the events of the story marked by tiny arrows: 'Here were wolves', 'Sunstroke', 'Royal Navy Rescue'.

In Michel Houellebecq's novel *The Map and the Territory* there are no illustrations; instead we are offered an intense description of the Michelin maps that push along the plot: '... the drawing was complex and beautiful, absolutely clear, using only a small palette of colours. But in each of the hamlets and villages, represented according to their importance, you felt the thrill, the appeal, of human lives, of dozens and hundreds of souls.'

In *Treasure Island*, Robert Louis Stevenson talks explicitly about the way a map engages the imagination, pulling you down into an undergrowth of daydreams. Jim Hawkins is sitting by the fireplace in the housekeeper's room, brooding over the pirate map of the island: 'I explored every acre of its surface; I climbed a thousand times to that tall hill they call the Spy-glass, and from the top enjoyed the most wonderful and changing prospects. Sometimes the isle was thick with savages, with whom we fought, sometimes full of dangerous animals that hunted us.'

Try that with a GPS.

There are plenty of other examples – the maps in Tolkien, or in *The Chronicles of Narnia*, or in Arthur Ransome books where, again, they record the events of the story ('Here they rescued a kitten'; 'Here they met a steamer in the dark'.)

For kids growing up in the Australian suburbs, maps were always part of your survival kit. They were not just maps. They were an escape plan. You could trace a finger on the road north, up into Queensland, until you found that intoxicating line dividing the desert from the fertile farmland: 'Notify police if you intend crossing this line.' Oh boy! The teenagers who lived there, by the edge of the desert, no doubt sat on their own beds, tongues stuck out in concentration, tracing the route to somewhere south.

Perhaps we can make do without a *Gregory's* but can we keep the other maps? They're the world's best open invitation.

The Renovation Rulebook

A friend has announced she is about to renovate her house. I have tried to dissuade her, pointing to the inevitable consequences of rage, bankruptcy and divorce. Unbelievably, she intends to carry on. Perhaps she – and others who are blithely considering renovating – need to study *The Renovator's Rulebook*. The following, anyway, is how it played out at our place.

Rule 1: Any drop of paint, released at ladder height will hit the one gap in your plastic sheeting.

Rule 2: Any step made backwards off a ladder will be into an open can of paint.

Rule 3: The only fabric you like will be the most expensive one in the shop. Ordering will involve a three-month wait.

Rule 4: The marital argument over whether to choose the 'Calypso Blue' or the 'Ocean Breeze' for the kitchen cupboards will rise in intensity according to the degree to which the two colours are indistinguishable.

Rule 5: The marital argument over whether to choose the 'Calico Horizon' or the 'Desert Sands' for the kitchen walls will be just as astonishing, which is surprising since both are identical shades of what used to be called 'off-white'.

Rule 6: The builder's initial estimate should be seen as a work of fiction so rich and imaginative that it could be entered in the Booker Prize for Fiction.

Rule 7: It's not true the builder will never turn up. He'll turn up on day one, at precisely the time promised, whereupon he will disconnect your plumbing, demolish a section of your roof, and remove your front door. It's then he'll disappear for six months.

Rule 8: Cans of paint come in quantities of 1 litre, 4 litres or 12 litres, while all Australian bedrooms require quantities of 1.2, 4.2 or 12.2 litres. This means there is no Australian shed in which you can open the door without hitting a 3-metre stack of old paint tins.

Rule 9: Every Australian man, when buying methylated spirits for a cleaning job, is required to say to the guy serving: 'Have you got any cold ones?'

Rule 10: Every Australian man when using a G-clamp, is required to say: 'It's just one of my many vices.'

Rule 11: Every Australian man when using a stud-finder before drilling a hole for a picture hook, is required to hold the tool against his own body and when the bulb lights up say, 'It's a very accurate device.'

Rule 12: All hardware items have strange Yorkshire-sounding names such as nondles, blurgins and grogans. This is to provide entertainment to people who work in hardware stores.

Rule 13: The builder will never listen to the radio station you listen to yourself: if you like ABC talk, he'll be on Classic FM; if you like Classic FM, he'll be on Triple M. Oh, and he likes it *loud*.

Rule 14: Important decisions are always made by the builder during the five minutes you are away from the site, including the decision to knock a hole for a window in the wrong wall and to pebblecrete the heritage-listed sandstone facade.

Rule 15: The height at which you place the door handles will seem a matter of enormous importance for the three days but will then never again enter your mind.

Rule 16: Cement dust, released by a builder at the far end of your backyard, will find its way into your underwear drawer by means still not understood by science.

Rule 17: The dollar figure – 'our absolute limit' – mentioned on the first day you walked into the architect's office will become a shameful secret, never again mentioned by either side.

Rule 18: The tool you need is always missing.

Rule 19: A telephone call always comes when you are atop a ladder with a loaded paint-roller. It is always a wrong number.

Rule 20: When working with electricity it's crucial to make sure you have everything you need. These comprise: an insulated screwdriver, a pair of wire cutters and life insurance.

Rule 21: The rubbish skip must by law be supplied by a company with a bad pun in its name, such as 'Skip the Tip', 'Hop, Skip and Dump' or 'Where'syourbin'.

Rule 22: If you live in Paddington or Prahran or Balmain you are required to paint at least one surface with the colour 'Hog's Bristle'.

Rule 23: If you live in Hawthorn or Haberfield, you are required to paint at least one surface with the colour 'Brunswick Green'.

Rule 24: If the whole room shrinks in hot weather, you've used too much wood filler.

Rule 25: Any improvement will make everything else look worse. 'If only we could get a new couch,' you say, but once you heave the glorious purchase into place, your eye will be drawn to the carpet, which used to look fine but now, with a brand-new couch sitting on it, appears to suffer from a medical condition. You then recarpet at which point your eye is attracted to the wall, which used to look fine but now ...

All Packed Up

The pre-peeled potato has arrived at our local supermarket, the perfect product for anyone just too busy to spend the forty seconds it takes to peel a couple of spuds. I wonder what they do with the forty seconds they save? Read Proust? Train for the Olympic squad? Knock out a few pelvic floor exercises?

The potato, in its natural state, comes equipped with its own packaging but, since this has been removed, a substitute plastic packaging must be added, the potatoes sitting nude and glistening on a black tray, clear plastic draped over the top like a see-through Doona. Since the aim seems to be a perpetual increase in packaging, I assume we'll soon end up with individual potatoes, each sitting on a sort of faux-velvet throw rug, to be viewed through a heart-shaped window, with built-in lighting and humidifiers.

On radio I was mildly critical of this development, only to receive a blistering text message in response. A chap with 'crippling arthritis' said the product was a blessing for those unable to use a peeler and I should take a good look at myself for what was essentially an attack on the disabled.

Fair enough but for some minutes I was distracted, trying to work out how he'd managed to be so instantly dextrous with a mobile phone keyboard – something I find almost impossible to use – and yet so defeated by a potato peeler. I conjured up an image of his twisted hands, the fingers jabbing angrily down on the keys, and decided it was, indeed, possible. Especially as his message was sent in ANGRY CAPITAL LETTERS.

Angry jabbing may well be easier than sideways peeling, requiring, as the latter does, pressure to be exerted sideways between the thumb and the forefinger. Once I have arthritis in my hands – instead of just everywhere else – I'll conduct an experiment and report back.

What I don't understand is why my arthritic mate thinks the plastic wrapping is going to be that easy to open. I find most plastic packaging impossible to open. Once, on a Qantas flight, I had a battle with a packet of peanuts all the way from Sydney to Perth. The packet won. Most of Australia's dental injuries are suffered by people attempting to gnaw their way into a bag of Burger Rings or breach the security cordon that is a Tim Tams packet. If they really wanted to protect the Green Zone in Baghdad they'd get Arnott's in.

Plastic, in so many ways, is a terrible form of packaging. It wrecks the environment, makes food sweat, and requires all sorts of chemicals to be added to stop the food turning grey. Plus you can't get into it.

That's why it's so frustrating to see its triumphant march through the fruit and veg section of the supermarket. Five years ago, lettuces were dominant. Most of the vegetable section consisted of lettuce. It sat in tall, majestic pyramids; Giza as depicted in leafy greens. Now, just a few years on, the lettuces cower in a single, sad pile, while bags of pre-packed leaves luxuriate in a refrigerated unit, spread along one whole wall. The bags, I note, are suitably puffed up, no doubt due to the speed of their conquest.

The apples are hanging on but they, too, are under challenge: a new product offers the convenience of pre-sliced apples nestling in a plastic bag. Presumably this is for people who have both arthritic hands and no front teeth and are therefore unable to either bite into the apple or cut it up.

What's maddening is our inability to take pleasure in the packaging provided by nature. Bananas, for example, come in a remarkable form of packaging called the banana skin, which protects the banana inside, allows the fruit to continue ripening and then changes colour, from green to yellow, to indicate when the fruit is ripe and ready to eat. Even better, it can be discarded and thence used as a prop in slapstick comedy.

As usual, we don't know how lucky we are and so the striptease continues: the carrot, the potato and the apple all asked to remove their perfectly good clothes and re-dress in synthetics. Even garlic, I noticed the other day, is now available by the bag, the cloves separated and peeled.

T.S. Eliot once asked the question: 'Do I dare to eat a peach?' To which the answer is now, 'Only if peeled, sliced, bagged and poisoned, and sold at a price per kilo double that of an ordinary peach.'

This, I suppose, is the way the world ends. Not with a bang but a weirdness.

Surprise Veganism

There has been much criticism of the declining standards in parliament yet our politicians are not alone. What about the etiquette crimes committed by the rest of us?

Phone abandonment
It's called a mobile phone because it's meant to be mobile. Why, then, do you leave yours on your office desk, where it rings almost constantly from the minute you leave the room, ceasing only when you come back in? And the ring tone? Isn't Crazy Frog a little 2004? The rest of the office looks at your unattended phone, endures the constant cacophony, and then glances over to the open window. Exactly how mobile could this phone be?

Elevator blindness
I can see you, standing there in the elevator, so how come you can't see me, running for the damn thing? Oh, you can pretend to be intently studying the control panel, as if the buttons were as complex as those in the

cockpit of a 747 and that you need to decide the precise level of thrust that will cause the lift to rise, but I'm wise to what's going on. You just don't want to wait the 3.5 seconds it will take for me to join you.

Eyejacking
I paid for the newspaper, so how come you're reading it? Sitting beside me on the bus, your sideways glance down towards my paper is so intense I find myself hesitating to turn the page lest you are not finished. Would it be easier if I just turned, faced you and summarised what Ross Gittins had to say in his last three pars? Would you like me to hurry up and get to sport? Perhaps you'd like me to hand it over so you can complete the crossword, I'm sure I have a pen you could borrow. Alternatively you could arrange your own bus-time entertainment like the rest of us.

Kneedling
This is the practice, restricted to males, of occupying two seats on the bus, much to the annoyance of others, by sitting with knees splayed wide apart. Oh, don't worry yourself; the rest of us will just stand so you can afford your testicles the airing they deserve on account of their pure size (at least in the tiny mind of their owner).

Edgehogging
I'm stuck on the F3, stationary in a five-kilometre queue of other motorists. None of us are happy. We are all in a hurry. So who is the person zooming up the breakdown

lane in a late-model BMW? A cardiac surgeon on the way to an emergency at Gosford hospital? A prospective new father with a wife in labour? No, just an egomaniac with an overpriced car.

Surprise veganism
I love that you are a vegan. And I'm sympathetic that your husband is wheat intolerant. And it's quite cute that your twin girls will only eat food that is white or, at a push, taupe. My point is that it would have been nice to know all of this at least a minute or two before I served the steak pie with Yorkshire pudding and bacon-infused spinach which I spent most of the weekend preparing. Next time I'll send a tick-list form and seek a medical history.

The etiquette horrors of our time? What a shame that it's good manners not to mention any of them.

The Broken Record

My father made it into the *Guinness World Records* in 1965, nestled alongside the world's fattest man, the world's smallest dog and the world's longest moustache. He was managing editor of Papua New Guinea's main newspaper, the *South Pacific Post*, when it received recognition as the world's 'Most Smoked Newspaper'.

As the entry explained, locals would mainly purchase the newspaper in order to roll cigarettes, for which purpose it was resold for sixpence a pound. In other words, 'incendiary prose', in the context of the *South Pacific Post*, was more a requirement than a compliment.

In a similar spirit, I mounted my own bid for inclusion in *Guinness World Records*; an attempt, if you will, to match my father's achievement. And like his record, it was more about quantity than quality. I attempted the world's longest interview, intent on smashing a previous record of twelve hours and thirty seconds achieved by Spain's Pedro Ruiz in Madrid in July 2009. I was ensconced in the window of an ABC shop with the most talkative person I could think of: the bandana-wearing author and former footballer Peter FitzSimons.

I interviewed him for twenty-four hours, from 10am one day to 10am the next, the encounter broadcast on digital radio.

This brought much chortling from friends and colleagues, who noted that with the voluble FitzSimons by my side victory was inevitable. They recommended the opening inquiry, 'Peter, tell us about yourself,' after which I would be able to slump into a meditative daze for the first five hours. I could then ask him to describe his greatest achievement on the rugby field, which would take care of the next fifteen.

My own plan was to soften him with easy questions for the first twenty-three hours and fifty-five minutes and then – with five minutes to go – hit him with the big one, 'Peter, the bandanna: why, why, why?' By this stage, I calculated, he'd be too weak to walk out on me.

The interview, strange to say, turned out a success. By the time we were seventeen or eighteen hours into it, we realised that people around the world were taking an interest.

Tweets and emails came in from people who were listening in Europe and South America. One bloke began listening in Sydney, flew to New Zealand and caught some more of the interview from his hotel room. Then, as we reached the 24-hour mark, there were more TV cameras, more radio interviews, a request to appear on *Sunrise* with Mel and Kochie, a message from someone who had just seen us on the news in Stockholm. Within a week, our stunt had been news pretty much everywhere. It had been what I believe news executives call 'the dancing monkey story' at the end of TV bulletins from London to North Korea: 'Meanwhile, in Australia, two morons ...'

'So what's the difficulty with that?' I hear you ask. Well, here's the problem. With this level of publicity, there's no way our record is going to last. Someone somewhere in the world is already thinking: 'Twenty-four hours, that's nothing.'

Around the world, publicity-hungry radio presenters will be surveying their contact lists and rating their nation's writers and academics according to volubility. At the BBC's Broadcasting House in Portland Place I hear a voice already shouting down a corridor: 'Can someone get me a number for Richard Dawkins?' At the Washington headquarters of NPR, my friend Scott Simon – never keen to be beaten – will be thumbing through his Rolodex, umming and ahhing between Alan Dershowitz and Garrison Keillor. 'Do you happen to be free?' he'll ask one of them. 'I have 1657 questions I urgently need to put to you.'

Celebrated windbags everywhere will suddenly be pressed into service for the honour of the nation. Certainly our appearance in the *North Korea Times* is a worry; North Korea doesn't like being beaten in these things. This is the country where one-time leader Kim Jong-il himself claimed a world record – alleging he had five times shot a hole-in-one during his first ever game of golf.

I now have a troubling mental picture of some unfortunate worker from Voice of Korea radio being held at gunpoint in front of a microphone, while a North Korean academic, similarly encouraged by a rifle poking into his ribs, is forced across the 24-hour line.

'I can't think of another question,' the interviewer will bleat at the 23-hour mark.

'I think you'll find you can,' the soldier will reply, idly flipping the safety catch on his rifle.

How long will our record last? A year? Two years? And if we are beaten, does that mean Peter and I, for the sake of Australia's national honour, will have to regroup and attempt forty-eight hours non-stop? The man, after all, hardly drew breath. Even after seventeen or eighteen hours, I found it quite hard to get a word in edgeways. 'Just let me clarify one thing,' I said during one of my occasional interjections.

'Richard, PLEASE ...' responded Fitzy, waving an admonishing finger, 'if you would just let me finish!!!'

In the end, North Korea, Britain and the US will be able to supply their own version of me, but will any other nation be able to produce a Fitzy?

Write On

The world is now full of writers' festivals and many young people are wondering how to break into the business so they can have the experience of jet-setting around the globe and being mobbed by grateful readers. Well, it's not good enough to just write a book; these days publishers will only consider something if it fits into an already successful genre.

The tendency began with the genre called 'chick-lit', which was invented in June 1995, when writer Helen Fielding noticed that her underpants were quite large. The effect was so startling in terms of book sales, the industry committed itself to only publishing chick-lit, or books from genres that at least sounded like chick-lit.

Just choose the genre that best suits your style of writing and the invitation to the free drinks won't be long coming.

Quick-lit

Modern printing techniques now allow the production of news-related books within minutes of an event occurring. Only a year or two ago, when Osama bin Laden's body was still sinking, having been dumped at sea, scores of publishers were already pressing the 'print' button. Of course, a book that has taken less than three hours to write may lack a little in the quality department but you'll be wowed by the speed.

Click-lit
This is a genre featuring books about the internet, all of them claiming the internet is about to kill off the publishing industry. It's a curious fact that the publishing industry would have died years ago were it not for the publication of thousands of books on the topic of how books are about to die.

Clit-lit
Eroticism for women, most obviously *Fifty Shades of Grey*.

Sick-lit
Crime books about ghastly murders in which whole chapters are dedicated to describing the crime, the state of the decaying body and the grisly process of the autopsy. No way is this sick and prurient; it's just that the central character happens to be a police pathologist ...

Dick-lit
Airport thrillers written for a male audience in which commandos, submarine officers or undercover spies save the day through acts of swaggering derring-do.

Crucially, something has to explode, sink or crash in the course of every page or, if possible, sentence.

Shtick-lit

Books written by comedians in which they work in their best lines, preferably while having a top-rating comedy show on TV. Jerry Seinfeld and Bill Cosby have each had their years in the sun; Tina Fey is the current champion.

Flick-lit

Any coffee-table book with lots of pictures and hardly any text, designed for people to flick through so they can feel cultured without having to actually expend any mental effort.

Sit-lit

This is the sort of volume perfect for reading when seated in the bathroom. My own book *The Dag's Dictionary* has made a modest contribution to the genre, yet nothing to match that of Jeremy Clarkson, who remains the world's leading provider of sit-lit, with a series of books featuring 950-word reviews of motor cars. Propped atop the toilet and aimed at the fifty-something male, a single Clarkson volume effectively creates a patriarchal cistern.

Tick-lit

Any book that promises to give you a tick of approval for views you already hold. Whole sections of the bookstore now consist of books for atheists that argue the case for atheism. This is a big shift from five years ago, when whole walls were covered in books about how George W. Bush was an idiot, expressly designed for people who thought George W. Bush was an idiot. The trick is to work out someone's opinion and then serve it back to them over the course of five hundred pages.

Kick-lit

Any sports book that claims to have been written by the sportsman himself but was, in fact, written by a grizzled ghost writer who spent five weeks recording conversations with said footballer trying to chance on a single coherent sentence.

Thick-lit

Fantasy novels, which, for reasons I've never understood, always have to be 600 pages long and part of a series of ten books with a pompous title like *The Agamemnon Chronicles*. Most bookshops can only now carry the work of about three authors, since just one series involves ten metres of shelving. As Mark Twain once said of a similarly hefty book, once you put it down, you can't pick it up.

Fitz-lit

Any book by Peter FitzSimons, each of which sells ten times more copies than any book of mine, leading me to a lifetime of bitterness and anger, and a tendency to sneak into bookshops and place a copy of my own dog-eared title on top of the stack of his.

And, finally:

Brick-lit

The only category that has now been removed from the Australian Publishers' Association-approved list. Alas, my own book about building a mudbrick house in the bush was so spectacularly unsuccessful, the whole genre has now been deregistered. So good luck. You'll need it.

Chapter 7

In which the world ends, but not before Paul Keating confronts the day and Hedy Lamarr presents her beauty tips

Safety Notes: Your New Ballpoint Pen

Everything these days comes with a lengthy brochure containing a series of safety warnings. Your new ballpoint pen is no different. Remember any failure to follow these warnings and cautions will immediately invalidate your warranty.

1. Do not chew the end of the pen as the plastic could shatter and become embedded in your lips.
2. Do not suck the end of the pen as the ink could leak and be ingested.
3. The plastic lid, if inhaled, could prove a choking hazard.
4. Do not use this pen in the middle of the night to write notes to yourself containing ideas of incredible brilliance which, upon waking, will imply you've been visited overnight by a leering madman with no discernible talent who enjoys leaving facile gibberish on your bedside table.

5. Do not use this product to write poetry unless you are (a) under sixteen; or (b) know what you are doing.

6. We make the point generally: the world has enough short stories.

7. Should a relationship be initiated through use of this product – including, but not limited to, the creation of a love letter, Valentine's Day card or other form of written inducement – the manufacturer will not be responsible for the cost of raising any resultant children, the purchase of a house in a *better* area close to a *good* school, nor the treatment of any sexually transmitted diseases contracted during the torrid affair you commence in order to distract yourself from this farce of a marriage.

8. The manufacturer does not recommend the placement of the pen in a plastic pocket protector, as this may cause others to label you a *nerd*, a *geek* or even a *maths teacher* in a way that may prove hurtful. Subsequent failure to form a meaningful relationship will not be covered under this or any future warranty.

9. The manufacturer is not liable for any loss of reputation should the pen be used to write the word *ironic* to describe a situation which is merely unusual, or to label someone *disinterested* when they are *uninterested*, or to say *my head literally exploded* when it did no such thing. To be honest, this stuff drives us

nuts. Oh, I know people say *it's clear what he meant* and *don't be such a pedant* but what's so hard about picking up a dictionary? These days there's one on your phone.

10. If working as President of the United States, or as the leader of any other major power, do not use this pen to start any further foreign wars. Of course, it's your right and in certain circumstances it may even be justified, but frankly we don't want to be involved. Just borrow a pen from someone nearby and it really would make a real difference to our anxiety levels about being involved in the pen business. Ahead of time: *Thanks for being so considerate of our feelings.*

11. If employed as a screenwriter, we really don't like the idea of you pitching anything with Mel Gibson. The way we see it, he's had his go. Loved him in *Braveheart* but recently he's been off kilter. If you must write a role for him, buy a pen from some other company. Or use a computer! We may lose some sales, but it's worth it to make a stand. Sorry but that's just how we feel.

12. If doodling with this device, the manufacturer recommends that you do not draw giant phalluses, severed heads or handguns with intricate cross-hatching, as this will shorten the life of the product by using up all the ink, and may result in people getting the wrong idea about your hobbies and interests.

13. Take your time using the product. Bring some elegance to your writing. God gave us the letter *q* so that the line would loop down like a fishing line cast into the sea. He gave us the letter *i* so we could imagine a small boy holding aloft a balloon, floating in a blue sky. I could spend a week talking to you about the calligraphic possibilities of the letter *r*. Instead what do we get? A lot of scribbling. Misspellings. Corrections. Weird doodles indicating sexual dysfunction. Cheques signed on accounts which are empty. (We shouldn't feel responsible but we do.) We put some effort into designing a good working pen. It was sold to you for $1.50. It's not like we are making a big profit. All we ask is that you do your part. Think before you use it. Use it for good not evil. Don't mix your metaphors. Don't insert either end into your ear. If you are using our pen to write a shopping list, include items high in dietary fibre. If using it to remonstrate with a junior staff member, be kind: the device in your hand can, in certain circumstances, be mightier than a sword. And for God's sake don't leave it in the pocket of your best shirt. If it leaks we're not paying.

Very Hot Mail

After a couple of decades writing a weekly newspaper column, I've had my first experience of an internet hate campaign. So far, more than 2,400 people, nearly all American, have emailed me. More emails come every time I hit the SEND/RECEIVE button. About five per cent contain threats of violence. Even stranger, quite a few threaten me with sexual violence. They say, in various ways, that they want to rape me.

The only good news: quite a few don't seem to know the precise location of Sydney. Or Sidney, as some call it. 'You are so out of touch with America, I cannot believe you are published by an American paper,' writes one emailer, having read the story on the *Sydney Morning Herald* website. Quite a few tell me I should be nervous if I ever try to leave Britain.

Here's how it started. I wrote a piece for the *Herald* about climate change. It was critical of both the left and the right and contained some comic hyperbole about both: that environmental zealots wanted us all to live in caves and that climate-change deniers should tattoo their beliefs on their bodies so they couldn't later deny their role in preventing action on climate change.

An extract:

Surely it's time for climate-change deniers to have their opinions forcibly tattooed on their bodies.

Not necessarily on the forehead; I'm a reasonable man. Just something along their arm or across their chest so their grandchildren could say, 'Really? You were one of the ones who tried to stop the world doing something? And why exactly was that, Granddad?' ...

Or what about their signed agreement to stand, in the year 2040, lashed to a pole at a certain point in the shallows off Manly? If they are right and the world is cooling – 'climate change stopped in the year 1998' is one of their more boneheaded beliefs – their mouths will be above water. If not ...

OK, maybe the desire to see the painful, thrashing death of one's opponents is not ideal. But, my God, these people are frustrating. You just know that in twenty years' time, when the costs of our inaction are clear, the climate deniers will become climate-denial deniers. 'Who me? Oh, no, I always believed in it. Yes, it's hard to understand why people back then were so daft. It's so much more costly to stop it now.'

That's why the tattoo has its appeal.

Not that the other side isn't frustrating. There's a type of green zealot who appears to relish climate change. Every rise in sea levels is noted excitedly. Every cyclone is applauded and claimed as a noisy, deadly witness for their side.

Suddenly, it's as if they have the planet's assistance in their lifelong campaign to bully everyone else into accepting their view of the perfect world. One without any human beings. Except for them. Living in a cave. Wearing an unwashed T-shirt that not only says 'Support wildlife', but actually does. ...

I then tried to identify why the left tend to believe in climate change, while the right sometimes doesn't, before concluding that the main thing was to acknowledge our best attempt at the truth – which is that climate change is occurring and we urgently need to do something about it.

So far, so ho-hum. On Saturday and Sunday, the piece failed to make it onto the *Herald*'s list of 'most read' opinion pieces. I had nine emails – four of them saying they agreed and five against, but all expressed pleasantly. No one thought the piece was offensive or even that remarkable. The comic hyperbole was seen as, well, comic hyperbole.

Then – sometime Sunday night – a link to the piece was put on a right-wing website in the US, offering me up as another communist trying to ruin the world through the 'hoax' of climate change. The piece started multiplying in cyberspace, mainly on websites dedicated to exposing the leftist conspiracy about climate change.

Suddenly I was the talk of the town: about 300,000 people read the piece on smh.com.au between Sunday night and Tuesday morning. I had more readers than anyone else in the *Herald*. Only problem was: many of them wanted to kill me.

I'm not going to argue that Americans don't understand irony; American comic writing can be sophisticated, sarcastic and subtle. Yet one of the dangers of the web is that writing with an English or Australian sensibility can be placed in front of an audience with a different tradition. When I write about tying a climate denier to a post off Manly so he can be consumed by the ever-rising waves, it was clear to an Australian readership that the image was meant to be comic and absurd. Indeed, in the original piece I explicitly call the notion 'not ideal'.

Clear? I thought so – but not clear enough.

My American correspondents believed I was seriously proposing they be tattooed against their will and tied to posts in the ocean. Given what they thought I was saying, I guess their upset was understandable.

And, boy, they were upset. TTB, from Nevada, said he had 'a couple of 9mm hollowpoints with your name on them'. Jonathan, of Sag Harbor, NY, wanted to remove my testicles, while DB wanted to remove my penis. And M Glasgow, in an email sunnily titled 'Can't wait to meet you', observed that: 'I will kill you so dead that your rotting body will do nothing but energise the worms and maggots that will do their part in saving the planet from morons like you.'

Actually helping nature through my own death is a theme that energises much of the correspondence. JH, for example, suggested that since I like nature so much, I should donate my 'otherwise worthless body to the study of marine life by serving as shark bait'.

Actually, that did make me laugh.

Many use the phrase 'you f---ing commie bastard', which seems charmingly retro. In others I'm a 'hardcore-Left ideologue and operative'. Stan, in Seattle, on the other hand, has me working for the British Royal Family: 'A whore working for the Queen's yellow green paper money'.

And a huge proportion mention Al Gore, whom they believe is paying me. So, boss, I need to tell you: they hate you even more than they hate me.

Apparently Gore has bought a beach property (in some emails he's bought two, in others four), thus proving he doesn't believe his own lies. Quite a few accuse me (and him) of working for what they call 'the Jews', and mention several big companies as having financed the hoax.

They are also pretty sure that I must be gay: 'a bitch on heat', who should 'take off your skirt and get a grip'. I probable drive 'a faggy little Prius' and am involved in regular 'teabagging' sessions with Al Gore – a term so new to me I had to look it up. Having done so, with all best wishes to Al, I think I'll pass.

And then, again and again, there are the guns: 'Keep talking crap and someone will surely shoot you!'; 'I have all the time necessary to put a well placed round in your vapid little head'; 'I'd be happy to blow your face through the back of your head with my shotgun'.

What wisdom have I drawn from the experience? Don't put an email address at the end of newspaper articles. Avoid travel in the near future to the American states of Arizona, Texas and Nevada.

And maybe, in a world of international publishing, learn to be clearer.

Boxed In

Ten or twelve years ago, I wrote a list of all the things I've learnt from watching TV. Many, I discover, are no longer relevant. It's no longer true that 'every office in America has a short, perky, libidinous redhead with kooky clothes and no apparent job' – not since the demise of both *Suddenly Susan* and *News Radio*.

I also can no longer defend the idea that every square metre of Sydney Harbour contains at least a couple of floating bodies. Ten years ago, watching Colin Friels at work in *Water Rats*, it seemed a miracle they managed to get the ferries through to Manly.

Nevertheless, if alien civilisations are monitoring our broadcasts, they'll still emerge with a quite peculiar picture. They'll now decide that all females on Earth work as pole dancers, save for one elderly woman in Britain, who is employed as a detective. And they'll note that even though vast quantities of television are produced, no one on television seems to watch the stuff.

They'll learn that nearly all bosses are working to subvert the work of their subordinates. And they'll note that when Earthlings go food shopping they return home with a single, large brown paper bag, out of which poke two French breadsticks or, occasionally, a bunch of celery. 'The Earthlings,' the final report would conclude, 'survive entirely on a diet of celery and breadsticks; their liquids consisting of drinks procured at pole-dancing establishments.'

So it's time for an update. Here's what I've learnt about life from another decade watching TV.

1. According to police protocol it is mandatory for all officers to meet their informants at a lap-dancing club, with a slightly-out-of-focus pole dancer in the background, bathed in red light.

2. In any hospital, a diagnosis delivered within the first forty minutes is sure to be wrong. Only with ten minutes to go is there hope the doctors might finally get it right.

3. Simply allowing Kevin McCloud onto a building site guarantees the glass won't fit.

4. Police officers are only ever able to solve crimes once they've been taken off the case.

5. The more brilliant the doctor, the more likely they're a socially abrasive curmudgeon.

6. The more brilliant the attorney, the more likely they're a socially abrasive curmudgeon.

7. The more brilliant the lie-detector psychologist, the more likely they're a socially abrasive curmudgeon.

8. When questioned by police, criminals like to keep their hands busy. That's why they're

always tinkering with a car, varnishing a yacht or brushing down a horse the moment the wallopers arrive.

9. Pretty much everyone in the US works either in advertising or architecture. The only known exception is Dan Conner in *Roseanne*, who always looked tired, presumably because he was the only gyprock installer in a nation of 307 million.

10. The mere presence of Bear Grylls in a locality guarantees the only form of sustenance will somehow involve faecal matter.

11. Groups of young, impoverished friends living in Manhattan always live in large, sprawling apartments with funky furniture, stylish objects and a good view.

12. Just mentioning that you are a Jehovah's Witness guarantees that, within four scenes, you'll require a blood transfusion.

13. The cafe table, restaurant booth or bar stool favoured by a person or group of friends always happens to be free the moment they walk in.

14. In any human interaction, the most important thing is always said just as someone is in the process of leaving the room, the proximity of a doorway allowing their thoughts to crystallise.

15. When people make a date to meet, they never need to nominate the time or place, the information being conveyed telepathically.

16. The fibre left at a crime scene never comes from a jumper bought at Just Jeans or Kmart. Instead, it's from a rare Belgian sheep whose fleece was sold to a company in Norway that manufactured club jackets for Mercedes drivers but only between January 1983 and April 1984.
17. Whenever anyone on the run enters a cafe, the TV in the corner is broadcasting news of their case.
18. Small towns are far more crime-ridden than cities, with the sleepy rural hamlet of Midsomer being awash with blood.
19. The chance of a character dying on a battlefield rises if he has only just reconciled with his long-lost mother/girlfriend/sister/cousin.
20. Women typically respond to impending danger by grabbing a torch and going outside to investigate wearing only a negligee.
21. The ability of a criminal to shoot straight decreases according to the importance of the cast member at whom he's shooting.
22. While accountants and psychologists are usually male, middle-aged and balding, by adding the word 'forensic' to the equation the person becomes twenty years younger, fantastically good-looking and female.
23. Chairs were so badly made in the Wild West, they immediately shattered when used in a bar-room brawl.

24. The fifty people talking loudly in the pub will kindly fall into a gentle hubbub once the main characters sit down and start to talk.
25. Melbourne consists of two suburbs – St Kilda and Fitzroy.
26. Sydney consists entirely of apartments with a view of the Sydney Harbour Bridge.
27. Or of the Sydney Opera House.
28. If in need of a replacement body organ, immediately make contact with your no-good long-lost brother, as he will prove to be the only person who is compatible.
29. In every drama there is a scene of the boss with some golfing equipment in his office, practising putting.
30. And, finally, the quality of the show plummets the moment you buy a season pass on iTunes.

The Submissionary Position

Sydney's Anglicans have changed the marriage ceremony so the wife agrees to 'submit' to her husband. People criticise the Sydney Anglicans for being out of touch, so how wonderful to see the success of *Fifty Shades of Grey* being rapidly reflected in the service. The only question: will fluffy handcuffs now be a mandatory part of bridal wear?

Jocasta has never agreed to submit in her life, unless you're talking about her stationery receipts, in which case she is annually submissive, but only to the Taxation Office. In all other matters, I deal with her as one would a madman wired with explosives.

I'm also unsure how this 'submission' thing works in practice. If it means Jocasta can no longer criticise my method of driving from Leichhardt to Newtown via Petersham, rather than her preferred method of up Parramatta Road and then right on Missenden, then I'm all for it. In my Anglican church-approved fantasy, I can hear the words of discontent beginning to form as I turn right into Crystal Street – Jocasta sighing, 'Not this way, again' – quickly brought to an end with my barked command of 'Submit, woman, submit!'

Presumably, the Anglican church has an arrangement with the riot squad to cope with the aftermath of my attempt to employ its ideas. I hear there's a fortified bikie clubhouse nearby, so maybe I could hole up there.

The church argues that families work best when they have a leader, and that the natural leader is the man. Australian women will be happy to accept this, according to the church, which, completely coincidentally, has a long history of believing in miracles.

Most men will like the idea of leading their family on an intrepid mission, even while acknowledging they need help locating their car keys and later asking for directions. With luck, even a woman who has 'submitted' would still be able to proffer her assistance in these matters.

If the Anglicans are going to change the marriage vows, it might be better that they moderate their expectations of both genders.

Given the obesity epidemic, we could pledge to stick by each other 'through thin – and thick', thus acknowledging our likely future shapes. And given the global financial crisis, we could include the pledge: 'Should one partner handle the superannuation, the other agrees not to mock the decision to get into iron ore, even though in retrospect it's bloody obvious the floor price was about to collapse.'

Children's names should certainly be settled during the ceremony. A simple yet elegant pledge – 'I agree to renounce any name previously employed by Posh and Becks' – could save a lot of heartbreak later.

The issue of faithfulness must be addressed. Monogamy might be difficult to achieve in this time of increased longevity, so why not set the bar at a more achievable level? 'I agree that should I have an affair it will be with someone fatter than my current partner.'

The breach of trust – you know it's true – will be easier to endure.

In a truly modern ceremony, the man would agree to never employ the word 'hysterical' during any matrimonial fight, while women would agree to turn a blind eye to the husband's consumption of the best part of a bottle of Coonawarra shiraz while watching the latest bonnet drama on the ABC, because drunkenness might be the only way for even a sensitive male to survive that much Thackeray.

Couples might also wish to tailor their vows to deal with particularly annoying personality traits. Jocasta might require my promise not to drive around on one-sixteenth of a tank of petrol, a failing that has led to a lifetime of us running out of petrol either (a) halfway across the Anzac Bridge, or (b) on bush roads in the middle of nowhere at 1.30am.

I, on the other hand, could request that she forswear the use of the female 'we', as in, 'Tomorrow, we are going to paint the fence,' which, when translated during the past thirty years, has always meant, 'Tomorrow, *you* are going to paint the fence.'

Overall, the aim is to peer forward into the marriage and foresee possible problems. Imagine the drop in the divorce rate if the marriage service included, as standard, the pledge: 'When playing the card game Five Hundred with my bride as my partner, I pledge not to comment on her staggeringly bold bids, and certainly pledge never to employ the phrase "What sort of idiot bids eight hearts without the right bower?"'

My point is that submission to the other person is not a bad idea. Just that it works best if both sides do it.

Paul Keating: A Day in the Life

Paul Keating opened his eyes to see bright light filtering through his bedroom window. He stared bleakly at the sun, regarding it with considerable contempt. 'A bloated puff-bag of gas, in the process of burning itself out,' muttered the former prime minister. A light breeze played through the window and he sniffed the air. 'Ah, yes,' he murmured, 'the poisonous miasma of a city of mediocrities.'

Keating swung his legs off the bed, touching his feet lightly on the cool wooden floorboards; floorboards, he took a mental note, as supine and downtrodden as the Labor Party under its current leadership. In a moment he would pad out in his dressing gown to pick up the *Sydney Morning Herald* from the nature strip. It would come in useful when the time came for his morning ablutions. He smiled at the thought. Mind you, his time in the bathroom hadn't been really pleasurable since Alan Ramsey left the paper.

In the meantime there was breakfast to consider. He would start with some muesli, as full of nuts and fruits as a party-room meeting of the Greens. To follow, he'd prepare scrambled eggs, as light and frothy as a policy statement by Andrew Peacock. Then some coffee – a dark and bitter swill – a representative swill you could say, in keeping with his mood.

A bird trilled in a tree outside his window. 'Typical,' P.J. jeered, 'a shrill, shrieking show-off, a carcass swinging in the breeze, only interested in feathering its own nest.'

He whimpered in disgust as he padded up the hallway. 'The way that bird is going on you'd think it was he who'd floated the dollar, removed trade barriers and single-handedly saved the nation.' The bird's trilling seemed to follow him up the hallway, like a dog returning to its own vomit.

It had been a disappointing few weeks. He'd personally redesigned Barangaroo, the new development area on the edge of the harbour, and yet the damned architects had been typically ungrateful. Didn't they realise his complete lack of experience or qualification in either architecture or town planning was an advantage? The Keating mind was at its most brilliant when unfettered by any actual knowledge. It had triumphed over the economy, save for a slight hiccup with interest rates; why not with town design?

A bowl of daisies sat on the kitchen bench, the buds struggling to open to the morning light. 'Gutless spivs,' observed the former prime minister as he wandered past.

The dust-up with the architects wasn't the only disappointment. There was the matter of Labor giving a cushy job to Peter Costello. Costello of all people – a policy vacuum so powerful he should have been sponsored by Hoover. Keating had Napoleon clocks with bigger tickers. Beazley, that slug, was off to Washington. Brendan Nelson, a man with more holes in his head than strictly necessary for his collection of earrings, was off to Brussels. And roaming around Rome was that dropkick Tim Fischer, a man whose brains would fall out if he ever removed that stinking affront of a hat.

Why hadn't Labor, during its time in office, crafted a job for P.J. Keating? It was a mystery beyond all reckoning. There must be something that suited his skill set. Head of the UN would do. President of Europe. Or, failing that, he could conduct Mahler in front of the Berlin Philharmonic.

He considered the contents of the fridge, spotting a tub of taramosalata and a bunch of rocket. That was the story of his refrigerator these days – it was all dip and no iceberg. He'd come a long way from Bankstown. As he searched for something to eat, his mind roamed back to the subject of architects. He hated architects almost as much as he hated Prince Charles, which put him in a quandary, since Prince Charles also hated architects. Was it okay to hate architects and Charles equally? Wasn't it said that the enemy of one's enemy was one's friend?

Various ancient hatreds did battle in the former prime minister's heart before settling into a truce. Charles probably hated the architects for a different reason from his own, some sort of contemptible reason that proved

Charles's idiocy, much as P.J. Keating's rather different reason proved his own brilliance.

A sigh of contentment escaped his lips. Thank God that had been resolved. Soon he'd need to face the day. Another day in which an ungrateful nation would miss the chance to fall to its knees and thank him.

He didn't expect much. Just a choral mass, involving the whole nation singing as one – from the mangy maggots of the right to the painted, perfumed gigolos of the left. Or perhaps they could organise themselves in the desert, all twenty-three million of them, spelling out the words 'We Thank You.' in letters stretching across the arid interior, Uluru itself forming the full stop.

He, P.J. Keating, Prime Minister of Australia 1991–1996, was big enough to ignore the personal faults of twenty-three million Australians, if only they'd do the right thing and mutter a 'thank you' that was somehow equal to his achievement. He opened the door and was hit by the smell of spring. It fair turned his stomach. He returned to his bedroom, closed the curtain and lay in the dark, daydreaming about the time he was king.

It was the regression he had to have.

The Hedy Lamarr Beauty
Program

Headphones, we're told, will soon be embedded in our ears, so no one need know that we are listening to our mobile phone or iPod. So far, so good, but has anyone considered the implications for the cosmetic surgery industry? From now on we may be able to avoid the knife and syringe by using sound – carefully chosen and discreetly delivered – to improve our appearance.

Consider the surgical operation known as the facelift. All it does is tighten your skin by exerting upward pressure, creating a permanent look of surprise as eyebrows are hiked towards hairline. With the new in-head technology the same effect can be achieved with a recording in which you are constantly told surprising facts.

'An elephant's penis is 1.5 metres long,' the voice might intone deep in your ear hole. Immediately the eyebrows elevate and the wrinkles disappear. It's natural, painless and involves an interesting fact that can later be used as a conversation starter.

'I bet you can't guess,' one might begin, 'the length of a typical elephant's penis ...'

Of course, Australia's cosmetic surgeons will have a thousand reasons why the new method won't work. What, they'll ask, if the world runs out of surprising facts? What if the person concerned knows all about elephant penises due to their employment at the local zoo, so much so they start debating the interesting fact in their own mind, saying, '1.5? Actually I think it's closer to 1.8', and assume a rather bad-tempered and wrinkly look as they enter the room?

And what if the fact is not so much surprising as discombobulating? A misplaced 'Hitler liked dogs' could cause the face to fall in a way that would emphasise, rather than reduce, the effects of gravity.

Timing, I think, is everything. Really surprising facts could be saved up for the moments you want to look particularly youthful. 'A crocodile cannot stick its tongue out,' the tape might murmur as you reach the doorway, not in itself an interesting fact but enough to get you focused. As you walk through the door, a few more facts, of increasing interest, delivered in rapid fire:

'The electric chair was invented by a dentist.'

'A Dalmatian is the only dog that can develop gout.'

'Virginia Woolf wrote all her books standing up.'

By the time you are through the doors, your eyes are wide and bright and your forehead is raised in astonishment: 'It's so surprising that she preferred this to sitting.' Instantly all your friends will think you've had work done. And good work too, mind, leaving no marks.

And should circumstances demand you look ten years younger – an old beau's wedding, a photo shoot for *Women's Health,* the chance of sex with a Sydney Swan – you could set your machine to deliver something so startling it cannot be true. 'Jim Morrison was born in a van but Van Morrison was born in a gym.' You'll find plenty of this gear on the web.

Of course, not everyone wants a facelift. Younger folk tend to prefer Botox, which stops wrinkles by freezing the face so it is left locked in a grim look of static distaste. Again, the new technology can help. Mere boredom can achieve that much sought-after 'Botox look'. A speech from the Assistant Treasurer. An Andrew Bolt column read aloud. Or just some intensely boring facts:

'Maine is the only US state whose name is just one syllable.'

'The first product to have a bar code was Wrigley's gum.'

'The highest Starbucks outlet is in Colorado.'

Thus assisted, what face would not be rendered into an immovable mask of sheer despair, similar to that adopted by some of our leading Hollywood stars?

Like any treatment, after-care is important. At the end of a night of surprising facts, it's important to allow the face to slowly return to its state of repose. On the trip home, the digital player could be set to 'returning to normal mode' in which facts of slowly dwindling importance would be imparted.

'"Stewardesses" is the longest word that can be typed with only the left hand.'

'Australia's capital city, Canberra, is 150 kilometres inland.'

'*Mad About You* star Paul Reiser played the piano on the show's theme song.'

By the time you climb into bed, your face will have returned to resting mode.

Of course, those who have simulated Botox will have to shock their system back into life. For this you may need to keep a truly surprising fact in reserve, much like heroin addicts keep on hand a store of naloxone. Confident our system will be widely adopted, we leave you with this final astonishing fact: please keep it somewhere safe and dry.

'A 1941 invention by the actress Hedy Lamarr, recognised by US Patent 2,293,387, is the basis of much of today's wi-fi and mobile communication.'

It's strange but true. Within a second, your lips will be curling into a smile while your eyebrows waggle upwards. It's the instant antidote to the aural Botox you took earlier – both stages delivered instantly and painlessly.

If I were a cosmetic surgeon, I'd give up now.

Now is the End

Every few months, someone predicts the end of the world. Are they mad? Perhaps not. It seems to me that certain things are on a trajectory. It's hard to see how they can go on this way. The end of days? The signs are all around us.

With thirty days to go ...
- Gina Rinehart's wealth keeps growing at the rate of $600 a second. As the end nears, she purchases a new sheep and cattle farm but keeps the traditional name: Victoria. Later she will also buy Greece, Italy, the United States ...
- The number of celebrities removing their clothes 'to raise awareness of breast cancer' grows to such an alarming degree that the former Scary Spice, Mel B, agrees to pose while fully clothed 'to raise awareness of modesty'.
- English becomes so laden with words that don't mean what people think, language itself *literally* ceases to exist, its speakers *disinterested* in ever saving it.

- Apple product launches become so ubiquitous there is one every two days, with men between the ages of twenty-one and thirty-four spending the majority of their lives queuing outside Apple stores. As soon as they reach the counter for one product, it's back to the end of the queue for the next. From their appearance – unwashed, feverish, mechanical in their movements – it's either the Apple queue or the zombie apocalypse.
- After twenty-five years of spellcheck, the population discovers it can no longer recall the difference between 'there', 'their' and 'they're', not to mention 'to', 'too' and 'two'. Written communication – first developed in Mesopotamia in 3200 BC – collapses in confusion.
- Ireland closes after it is revealed the entire population is overseas, performing in Riverdance.

With twenty days to go …
- The number of TV talent shows continues to grow until every Australian is a contestant in at least one program, all of us appearing on the same night. The lack of anyone at home to vote creates a financial tsunami, destroying much of the Australian stock market.
- Miniaturisation proceeds at such a pace that, within days, smartphones, laptops and iPods become so small they cease to exist. People

reach into their pockets, search around and realise there's nothing there. All the world's communication ceases save for some face-to-face grunting.

- Office workers spend so much time dealing with their emails each morning that they are still going at 5pm, deleting unwanted messages about the routine maintenance shutdown of the air-conditioning in the Brunswick sub-office, and are thus unable to do any actual work. The impact, if any, remains unclear.

- Social pressure forces everyone to join a baffling number of social media websites – 'But surely you're on Pinterest?' – with the result that people no longer have time to wash themselves. Disease begins to spread.

- Gossip magazines focus on fewer and fewer celebrities until every single article is about Kate Middleton (or, at a push, her sister's bottom). Even readers of *Who* magazine find this so dull they fall into a mass hypnotic slumber.

- Muffins continue to grow in size until they can no longer be lifted by retail staff, operating as they do under strict health and safety rules. Hungry crowds gather at shop counters to nibble at the edges of the immovable morning treats.

- The fashion world runs out of periods to revive. The '70s, '80s and '90s have all been done. Periods that have only just ended are revived.

One week they'll revive the week before. Then it will be the day before. Then the hour before ...

With ten days to go ...

- Food trends become so ridiculous that a handful of activated almonds stage a co-ordinated attack, teaming up with some annoyed organic spirulina.
- A Russian general trying to series-record Chris Lilley's new comedy on his Foxtel iQ – in breach of the territory block – becomes confused and launches a first-strike nuclear attack on the US.
- The urge to photograph your breakfast and send it out via Instagram becomes so intense, the world's mobile-phone systems collapse. Pockets of civilisation remain among those few who can still remember how to use a landline.
- Hollywood collapses after executives realise they have run out of Marvel comics to remake.
- A Dutch reality-TV show presents cannibalism in a *Ready Steady Cook* format. Producers, no longer able to undercut each other in terms of taste, leave the industry and reality TV ceases to exist. The citizenry, left unoccupied for hours each evening, turn to civil disobedience, and rioting breaks out in our major cities.
- The self-checkout machines at supermarkets become self-aware and go on the attack, accusing all of humanity of being 'an unexpected item in the bagging area'.

- Popular culture becomes so self-referential it creates a vortex and disappears into itself, thus ceasing to exist.
- My Family stickers become standard on most cars.
- Men's pants that show off their ankles become commonplace.

The end cannot be far off ...

Pat the dog and kiss your children. It's not the end of the world, but you can certainly see it from here.

Chapter 8

In which shampoo is
abandoned and an
optimist's errata is
compiled

An Optimist's Errata

I'm sitting on a North Coast beach reading Margaret Atwood's new novel, a book oozing with anxiety about the imminent breakdown of civilisation. Frankly, I'm finding it difficult to concentrate as I keep getting distracted by the happy laughter of the people around me.

I put the book aside and pick up a tabloid newspaper, but its worldview is strangely similar. According to a quick scan of the first three pages, there's hardly a young person in the country who isn't running amok with a gullet full of pills and armed with a pump-action shotgun. The only exceptions are those rendered so unfit by obesity that they find running amok simply too exhausting.

It's true – the beach in summer may not be the best place to take an accurate snapshot of society. All the same, from where I'm sitting – on one of those legless beach chairs – the pessimists do seem to go on a bit.

It's striking, for a start, how little this scene has changed over my lifetime. Families play beach cricket, older teenagers gambol in the surf, and younger ones bury their long-suffering fathers in the sand, all using time-approved methods. The whole scene represents a happily unchanging Australia, the existence of which is hardly ever acknowledged in either the tabloid media or the literary novel, both of which prefer the Chicken Little-style of reportage, one that involves running around squawking 'the sky is falling, the sky is falling'.

It's true that parts of the sky sometimes appear a little shaky due to global warming ... but could we spare a few centimetres of print to note that other sections of the firmament remain relatively intact?

I hardly see a computer game during my week up here. The main handheld entertainment device goes by the name of a 'fishing rod'. You see them everywhere. A good tabloid paper would do a story about it: 'Fishing epidemic among young people. Experts warn about overuse affecting arm ligaments and dangers of too much fresh air'.

Every bridge is lined with kids, all happily chatting and fishing. I wander past one child – six or seven years old – who has just pulled up a net full of tiddlers. 'Holy smokes, Jarryd!' he yells to his friend, 'we've got moollions of them.' He looks up at me. 'You want some mullet?' he asks, his voice spluttering with excitement. He dances from foot to foot at the pure thrill of it and then slips the tiny, silvery fish back into the water. He's like a kid from Norman Lindsay's *Saturdee* or *Redheap*, even if in the twenty-first century the best mate is called Jarryd rather than Waldo or Jacko, and even if he has mucked up the traditional idiom, which last time I heard was 'holy smoke' not 'holy smokes'.

Later, up the road, I see a father and son in the supermarket debating the relative merits of the single-plugger versus the double-plugger thong. Ah, that timeless Australian talking point. In the end, they decide – as have thousands of Australians before them – the extra reinforcing on the double-plugger is worth the additional fifty cents.

Others remain thongless and dance the traditional hot-sand cha-cha as they proceed from car park to beach, going 'ah, oo, ah, ah, ah' like a troupe of back-up singers. The mothers chorus back, chanting from their collective Jungian memory, 'It's not that hot. You'll be right.'

At the picnic ground, gathered around the barbecues, are small groups of various ethnicities. Each appears to consist of a father, a mother and two or three teenage children. Not one of the fifteen-year-olds appears to have a heroin needle in his arm, nor is any currently downloading pornography. Some may be wearing single-pluggers, I just can't say. The only weaponry being carried by the various groups is tongs.

Kangaroos graze. There's the tinkle of laughter. Everyone is drinking responsibly. No wonder nobody has ever bothered to record this scene.

Later in the week, I plunge into the new novel by DBC Pierre, the Australian-born writer who won the Booker Prize for *Vernon God Little*. Like all prize-winning novelists, DBC believes the Western world is in a state of terminal decline. His new book starts with a guy deciding to commit suicide and continues downwards from there.

I have interviewed the author on radio, and he seems rather jolly, his eyes sparkling merrily as he talks. Not for the first time, I wonder about the sincerity of this grim view of the world. When a literary novelist wakes up in the morning, does he or she really believe the world is a detritus-strewn capitalist battlefield with a hollow bleakness at its core? Or are they just bunging it on?

For their sake, I hope they are just bunging it on. The London of Martin Amis, for example, is so full of crime and violence that you'd hardly dare put a foot out your own front door. Maybe he doesn't. And the dystopias of Margaret Atwood are so hideous, you'd really be better off ending it all now.

Which is what DBC Pierre's main character decides to do. But not, I note, the writer himself.

Does it give them pause that this horrid, crime-strewn world is the same as that conjured up by tabloid media? There's a murderer at the bottom of every street and a rip-off buried in every deal; bureaucracy has always gone mad. We think it's a form of blindness when *A Current Affair* sees the world through this limited lens, but the same one-eyed quality seems to be rewarded when packaged as literary fiction.

Of course, there are some pretty rotten things about the modern world. DBC Pierre, for example, spends quite a few pages on the difficulty of buying a rail ticket in modern Britain. I've had the same experience and it is very annoying. My question is whether the differential pricing of rail tickets in Britain is an accurate metaphor for the existential horror of life itself. Ditto the scene in which the main character becomes lost in a giant IKEA store.

If these petty annoyances are to be included in literary novels, shouldn't they find space to record the petty pleasures of life? The great novelists of the nineteenth century – Balzac, Dickens, Tolstoy – castigated their society and yet always found room to explore the pleasures of, say, a well-cooked meal or the glimpse of a young lady's leg.

Maybe the current crop of literary novels could include a slip of paper, an optimist's errata, tallying the small pleasures the novelist neglected to include. Some suggestions:

The cheapest breakfast – home-cooked porridge – tastes fantastic, costs ten cents a serve and is good for you; hotel lifts these days tend not to feature muzak; and the micro-mini is back in fashion, oh, thank you, Lord.

Driving on the busiest road, it's rare to wait more than a few seconds for someone to be kind enough to let you in. Cheap airfares mean that everyone, not just the rich, gets to travel. And crime in most of the Western world is going down, not up.

While it's true we live in a materialist age, most people understand that consumerism does not bring happiness. Yes, we all rushed out and bought a flat screen television, but not because we are spiritually empty husks of humanity trying to find succour in an alienated world. We just thought the picture was better.

It's been raining in the wheat belt. You can buy a terrific bottle of wine with the pay from an hour's work. The beach is free.

Flat-pack furniture doesn't last forever but for young couples setting up a house for the first time, it's not bad value for money. The generation gap is smaller than it's been for generations; parents and children generally like and even admire one another. Homophobia is lessening. We're becoming more sensible about mental illness.

The supermarket is full of packaged-up crap, it's true, but look in most people's trolleys and dinner still means fresh food – chicken and salad; chops and veggies. The vast majority of people try very hard to be good parents.

Google is great. Cars are much safer than they used to be. The ability to pay your bills online is a huge convenience.

The sun still shines. The tap water tastes terrific. Most people in the world are honest.

Privacy, it's true, is being chewed away by the internet and social media, but with uncertain results. Hypocrisy and prejudice may be a bit harder to maintain in a world in which so many secrets are on display.

The new Amanda Palmer album is a blast. With the help of a credit card, I bought replacement handles for all my old saucepans – home-delivered for less than $25. How easy was that? And the last time we went to the casualty department of our local hospital, they saw us within the hour.

And, while we're searching for positives, DBC Pierre's new book is not a bad read. As long as you don't expect it to tell you how life really is.

Back at the beach the next day, I catch two good waves after lunch before being badly dumped. I struggle to the surface as another wave crashes into me. Momentarily blinded and putting up my arms for protection, I find my outstretched hands neatly cupping two well-rounded breasts. Naturally, I'm mortified. It's sure to be some poor nineteen-year-old girl who will be awfully upset. I open my eyes and discover the breasts belong to a somewhat pudgy nine-year-old boy. I fight off the urge to say, 'Nice set, mate,' and instead make an apology.

'Sorry, mate.'

'No worries, mate,' he answers unconcerned, swimming off.

Yes, it's all pretty sunny up the coast, whatever the alarmists say. Although they may have a point on the topic of childhood obesity.

The No-Shampoo Challenge

Spending a night at home in front of the TV is like being locked in an abusive relationship. Every ad break, you are the target of some sort of monstrous slur. 'You're fat,' says the ad for the weight-loss centre. 'Your skin is all blotchy and yuck,' chimes the ad for the cosmetic company. 'And, plus, you smell,' agrees the ad for the deodorant.

It's then back to the TV program for a few moments until it all starts again. 'Your teeth are gross. Your house is so germy that you've endangered your children. And – oh my God – you really *should* do something about your breath.'

Well, pardon me. All I was doing was sitting here on the couch watching a bad detective show and this is the thanks I receive from the advertisers. I feel like answering back: 'You are not a good person. You're just trying to make me feel bad in order to sell me some crap I don't need.'

This, as we all know, is how advertising works: it tries to make you feel bad and insecure and then – what do you know? Voila! – the company reveals it has the perfect solution to the insecurity it has just managed to create. Advertising is like a Mafia extortion racket: it offers protection from a menace of its own making.

Witness the number of products designed to stop us smelling: soap, shampoo, deodorant, perfume, odour-eaters, toothpaste, mouthwash. The only way to sell them is to convince us that our bodies would be putrid and repulsive if we didn't make active daily use of them all.

Is this true, though? A few years ago I launched the No-Shampoo Challenge on my radio show, stealing an idea from the British political journalist Matthew Parris. Together with more than 600 volunteers, I tested what would happen if we simply discontinued our use of shampoo. Shampoo, the theory goes, is simply a detergent that strips the natural oils from your hair. The human scalp then responds by producing more oil to replace that which has been lost, forcing the hapless consumer to use more shampoo, much to the delight of the shampoo company. Stop using the stuff and your hair will get greasier and greasier for about six weeks but will then reach equilibrium, after which you'll march into a sunny upland in which your hair will look terrific, smell terrific and you'll never have to use shampoo again.

And here's the thing, we found the theory was correct: over eighty per cent of the volunteers reported their hair was the same or better than it had been with shampoo. It's true not all 600 stuck with the new regime after the experiment ended, but many did. They come up to me all the time – on the street, at music gigs – and invite me to smell their hair. It's an invitation that requires some explaining to others who may be present. I've also stuck with it myself: five or six years on, I wash my hair with hot water under the shower but never use shampoo. If this book had scratch-and-sniff technology I'd invite you to lean closer and inhale deeply. You'd find my hair, I guarantee, to be sweet smelling.

A whole product range proved unnecessary. A whole aisle of the supermarket that can be ignored. But, soft, another challenge approaches.

The New York Times reports a new movement in the United States. This one is called the No-Soap Challenge. Under the headline 'The Great Unwashed', we meet Americans who have decided to go without deodorant and, in some cases, soap. The paper cites a book called *The Dirt on Clean: An unsanitized history*, which argues that since the advent of cars and labour-saving machines, 'we have never needed to wash less, and we have never done it more'. And it quotes scientists who claim that just as the stomach contains good bacteria, so our skin is alive with beneficial germs that help maintain healthy skin.

Back in Australia, the fashion researcher Tullia Jack is part of the nascent movement; she asked thirty volunteers to each wear a pair of jeans for three months without washing them. The jeans have been on display at the National Gallery of Victoria in an exhibition called *Nobody Was Dirty*. The jeans smell 'human',

Jack says, but not actually bad. And tests show they are not carrying a heavier-than-normal load of germs.

Civilisation moves forward through the efforts of a handful of visionaries: people who endure the mocking of the crowd in order to free the world from ignorance. First there was Galileo with his reimagining of the universe. Then there was me with the No-Shampoo Challenge. Now there is Jack and her dirty jeans.

On the other side of the barricades are those who are increasingly phobic about germs. Soap, for instance, is full of germs, according to *Australian House & Garden* magazine, which recommends every member of the household, as well as any passing guests, be given a personal bar of soap with their name carved into it. This is so clearly bordering on clinical insanity, I have an urge to ring the mental health hotline and demand some sort of intervention.

Presumably, soap being soap, the names have to be re-carved every night, each person bent over their sudsy palimpsest, vainly trying to fix their moniker on the ever-shrinking tablet. I just want to know: are family members sharing tools? And how high is the risk of a soap-related injury?

So many questions. Luckily, one of the advertisers in the same magazine comes to the rescue about a page later, with the alarming headline: 'Do You Know Where Your Soap Has Been?' It then presents a 'diary of a dirty bar of soap', suggesting you should worry about using the same soap as other members of your family. The conclusion? You should invest in a pump-pack container of soapy stuff. (Product slogan: 'Taking money off sad and phobic customers for over a generation'.)

Have people gone completely mad? How have I survived this long despite my wayward and foolhardy use of soap? At the very least, it's now clear I should always use a second bar of soap to soap the soap before I use it as soap.

Which brings us back to the advertising industry and its effort to make us believe we are smelly and repulsive and unpleasant. Quentin Crisp, the writer and raconteur, argued that if you never dust your apartment the dust gets no worse after the third year. We now know that's also true for the hair on one's head and the jeans on one's bottom. With sufficient courage, freedom can be ours. All we need to do is choose a place for the first mass meeting of our new political movement.

Outdoors, I think, would be best.

A Muddy Sisyphus

Sisyphus is the fellow in Greek legend required to push a large rock up a hill, whereupon it would roll down and he'd have to push it up the hill again. For. All. Eternity. He is, of course, the mythological figure that comes to mind when many of us contemplate our day-to-day lives, but there's one thing worse than a Sisyphean task and that's the task you do a million times before finally figuring out the right way to do it.

And here's the horror: once you work out how to do it, this particular challenge seems to immediately disappear from your life.

At the mudbrick compound I've been building in the bush, I've spent twenty-five years making mudbricks, mostly with the sole assistance of my co-builder, Phil. Over the years, friends have occasionally come up to help but only the once. At the end of a weekend of brick-making, they hobble back to their cars, unable to stand up straight and slightly dizzy with sunstroke, after which they tend to break off all contact. Short of being arrested for a hate crime, there's no better method of losing all your friends than inviting them to make mudbricks.

The traditional method of making bricks was designed by chiropractors in the early fourteenth century as a way of whipping up trade. Every step in the process involves maximum pressure on the small of the back – digging the dirt, mixing the mud, then making the bricks. Over the years, we have made 5454 mudbricks. You'll notice my precision about the number: the pain involved in each allows for no rounding up or down. And so, imagine the pleasure when we realised we only needed 400 more bricks to complete our second and final building. After a quarter of a century, we were about to make our last batch of bricks.

At this point, one of our bush neighbours wandered over. He mentioned that he owned an old electric concrete mixer. Connected to the generator we'd recently purchased, maybe it could provide some assistance in the business of making mudbricks. Who knows? It's got to be worth a try.

Perhaps, at this juncture, we could return to Sisyphus. We left him pushing the rock up the hill only to see it roll down again. I imagine him, labouring under the hot Aegean sun, having a sudden thought: why not introduce a second rock and a counter-weighted pulley system, through which the whole process could be automated? He'd be about to commence construction when a second thought would strike: even better, how about putting a chock under the rock at the top, thus stopping it from rolling back?

Sisyphus would give it a go, inserting the chock and watching in excitement as the rock held firm on the top of the slope. 'Damn,' he'd say as he wiped his brow, 'if only I'd thought of this chock idea way back at the beginning of time. Think of all the effort I'd have saved.'

It's at this point the voice of Zeus would boom through the clouds: 'Sisyphus. You might as well let it roll down again. Actually, I'm kind of over the whole rock thing; I mean, who really cares?'

Sisyphus would then throw himself off the mountain. The endless, pointless labour was one thing, but the pain of knowing it had been avoidable ... now that's punishment.

Thus we return to the matter of the bush block and the concrete mixer. The mixer, I discovered, halves, perhaps even quarters, the labour involved in making the bricks. The task it removes, that of hand-mixing the mud, is by far the most pain-inducing and time-consuming. The resultant mud is also vastly superior. The bricks are easier to make and more pleasing to the eye. Meanwhile, I also worked out how to use a small solar pump to bring water from the dam up to the mud pits. After twenty-five years of donkeying buckets of water up the hill, I'd used my brain instead of my back and alighted on the most obvious of solutions.

We made the final 400 bricks in a single weekend. If we'd used these methods from the start, we would have finished our building about fifteen years ago and would still possess friends.

Maybe all of life is like this. Australian governments will only work out how to receive proper value from the sale of public assets when selling the last of them. The moment you find a good hairdresser is the moment you lose all your hair. Don't learn how to tie a bowtie or you'll never be invited to a fancy function again.

Sisyphus is all very well. But we need a new mythological figure: one destined for all eternity to figure out life's tasks, just at the point they no longer need doing.

The Christmas Commandments

And the Lord contemplated Christmas and he became sorely aggrieved. He said, 'It was only ever meant to be a simple birthday party. How did things get so out of hand?' And so the Lord made new laws to get things back on track.

And the Lord said: 'Should you wish to send a greeting card to mark the season, let not that card be marked by bragging, even unto the brand of car you have purchased, though it be a Merc or possibly an Audi. And though great be your jubilation about your daughter Chloe, who won the Year 5 music prize with her cello, do not go on and on about it, especially if the woman who receives the card also has a Year 5 daughter, but hers was arrested for shoplifting. And though vast be your joyousness in your partner whose salary, including bonuses, now resembles a mountain of gold that glints like a thousand eyes, careful shall you be in the expression of these things, saying simply, "We're all well and hope you are too."'

And the Lord said: 'And should you become sorely tired writing the same message in a great multitude of cards, and should you think, "I know, I will just write one long message, four or five pages, closely typed, print it many times and then place a copy in each card so all may know the news from my family, even unto the cost of the dog's operation," then verily should you think again.'

And the Lord said: 'And should you find yourself in the shopping mall with your left blinker on, waiting for a car park, when all the other spots are taken, and verily does a lady zip in and take that very spot, though you'd bagsed it, that much was clear to all, let there not be lamentations in which the air is rent with fury, and let not the lady driver be smote with terms such as "abomination" and "evildoer" and "bloody Volvo driver". Instead, cast your eyes to the horizon, whereupon will appear another shopper, pushing a trolley resplendent with gifts. Follow this man, as a lion would follow a wildebeest, and verily, in time, his spot will be yours.'

And the Lord pondered. And the Lord cleared His throat. And the Lord pulled at His right ear lobe to assist His thought process.

Then He spoke, His voice low and steady, for this was the important bit: 'And once inside the shopping mall, let not one man fight against his neighbour, though both have one hand on the Giggle and Hoot Hootabelle Pillow, and it be the last such item in all of Sydney, even unto the Central Coast, and it hath been keenly requested, on the one hand by Samantha, aged four, and on the other by Timothy, aged four, and tremendous will

270

be the tumult on Christmas Day on the part of him or her who does not get it, with the gnashing of teeth and the kicking of legs; yet desist, I say to you both, from pulling this way and that on the pillow, saying, "It's mine," and "No, it's mine," until the fabric be sorely strained and the Giggle and Hoot Hootabelle Pillow be finally rent in twain, the store filled with a stuffing that floats on the air like pestilence.'

And then the Lord turned His mind to the day itself. And he spake thus: 'Bless the little children and keep them from sugar, especially buckets of it in the hours before breakfast, for its consumption will turn them into a mighty wind that will rush through your home and the fruit of this wind will be pain and its tune will be the sound of breaking glass.

'And verily should the wine not be opened until 11am, and even then a tiny sip of champers, just to get in the mood, lest the wine extend its dominion over the whole day, nourishing the evil in men and causing Uncle Michael to mention Uncle Terry's legal difficulties, which all agreed would not be mentioned.'

Then the Lord said: 'And lo, you shall read the recipe to the very end and understand that a big turkey takes time and you can't just defrost it by putting it under the hot tap for five minutes and then expect the oven to do the rest, even though you haven't even started by 11.30am. What were you thinking?'

And God became a little maudlin and thought about how all He'd wanted was a simple celebration. Who would have guessed everyone would get so tense, spending a whole month moaning and whingeing and talking about 'being under pressure' and 'there's so much to get done', and saying – this was the hurtful bit – they wished Christmas was over before it had begun.

God sighed. Sometimes He wondered whether anyone liked Christmas except for the five-year-olds. Then again, He thought to himself, they *really* like it.

At that God smiled. Then He decided to add just one more rule. A great shadow passed across His brow and His voice shook like thunder.

'Socks,' He said. 'Just remember. No one wants socks.'

New Year's Eve: Viva La Resolution

In the coming year I will drink less.

In the coming year I will eat less.

In the coming year I will exercise more.

In the future year when writing emails, I will employ at least some of the good manners that I once used when composing handwritten letters, including using initial capitals on people's names because, well, they deserve it.

I will pay off my credit card on time.

I will attend the doctor.

I will floss my teeth.

In the year ahead, I will also not take offence when my partner criticises some small aspect of my behaviour, for instance my tendency to throw my slightly damp bath towel on the matrimonial bed, suppressing the urge to respond as if her small criticism amounts to an attack on my slovenly attitude to household chores in general, my standing as a human being and, indeed, our entire life together, 'which clearly means nothing to you, nothing at all, what with the towel and everything, and given you hate me so much, you really might as well go and stay at your mother's, since ...'

I will eat my greens.

I will have the car serviced.

I will harass the bank until it gives us a better rate.

I will leave my car keys every evening in a bowl that I shall place on the kitchen bench so that my departure each morning will be calm and ordered and loving – 'See you when we both get home' – and not a scene of frantic shouts and pleading for assistance and unpleasant accusations against my partner as to 'Where have you bloody hidden them?' and 'I suppose you think this is a joke'.

I will drink six glasses of water each day.

I will swallow five millilitres of fish oil each day, though the subsequent burps would kill a brown dog.

I will sort my CDs and give away those I no longer play.

As the old year gives way to the new, I will learn to be calm when aggravated.

I will save all our photos on some sort of separate memory thingo so we don't lose everything when the computer goes bung.

I will learn one good joke.

I will stop drinking coffee after lunch because I know it means I'll wake up at 3am and be unable to fall back to sleep due to dire thoughts about Australian politics, the state of the world, and the personal failings of almost everyone I know, including myself, in fact *especially* myself, when really it would have been simpler to just have a cup of tea.

I'll give more to charity.

I'll read Montaigne.

I'll try not to be so noisy when I chew.

I will stop eating food straight from the pot as part of the process of washing up, acknowledging that the phrase 'waste not, want not', while useful in principle, is not so useful in practice – not when the method of preventing wastage is to insert all available leftovers into the stomach of a middle-aged man of already-fading attractiveness.

I will compare green slips.

I will be cheery at work.

I will email my cousin.

I will endeavour to more closely interrogate the reasons for consuming my fifth drink of the night, acknowledging that my previous rationalisations – 'it's been a bad day at work', 'it's been a good day at work', 'it's been rainy', 'it's been sunny', 'Tuesday only comes once a week', 'the dog has fleas' etc. etc. – may, in the fullness of time, be seen as nightly acts of consecutive self-delusion.

I will plant vegetables.

I will say please.

I will say thank you.

I will take all the socks from all the various drawers, and locate a twin – wherever a twin exists – and dispose of all the single socks, which for decades now have been building up in the laundry basket to such an extent that the addition of a single shirt fills the thing to the brim.

And, finally, I will go to a New Year's Eve party and behave myself, not talking too much, not drinking too much, not making a pig of myself with the guacamole, not pretending to remember people in circumstances where I haven't the foggiest, and not flirting with my partner's best friend from school, saying, 'Why don't you come over and sit here?', patting the spot on the sofa next to me, my face red with wine and sweaty in a way that's quite off-putting, and all this while trying to remember to leave time to run through my New Year's resolutions.

Which, given their number and urgency, I may need to start reciting about now.

A Fine Whine

Could someone please republish A.B. Facey's *A Fortunate Life* and hand it out at railway stations? In the course of its pages, a nuggety Aussie bloke battles through poverty, the Depression and two world wars and comes up smiling. There's no winking cleverness in the title. At the end, he really does believe he's had a fortunate life.

Meanwhile, the richest generation of Australians that has ever existed can't stop moaning. Remember the old joke about a planeload of Poms landing at Mascot? The engines are switched off but you can still hear the whining? That's now us.

Politicians vie with each other to convince us no one is worse off than we are. We are surely the most miserable people on the planet, they seem to imply, and certainly worse off than any Australians who have come before us.

The sounds made by our politicians are increasingly those of a mother comforting a toddler who had scraped his knee.

'There, there,' one side says, 'it must really hurt, what with the petrol prices and the road congestion.'

'Yes, yes,' says the other, applying a band-aid to the collective wound, 'it must be terrible, what you are going through.'

This said while Pakistan was crippled by flooding, Afghanistan was being shot to pieces, and half of Greece seemed to be unemployed. Yet we're still the ones who need a little sympathy.

And it's not only the politicians. Every second letter to the paper starts with the proposition that the country is going backwards. The correspondents have different explanations of why this is so – the refugees, the education system, the existence of young people – but no one challenges the starting point: that life in Australia is worse with every passing day.

This is not to mock the difficulties of making ends meet on a limited wage or the challenges of unemployment, living with a disability or myriad other mountains people must climb. Yet these are problems faced by every generation. They're worse elsewhere. They've been worse here. People – like A.B. Facey – somehow endured life's shortcomings without thinking themselves uniquely mistreated. Well, not here, not now. Which of today's politicians or opinion makers would dare repeat Malcolm Fraser's statement of the obvious: 'Life wasn't meant to be easy'?

Listen to the sound of talkback radio and it's like Senna the Soothsayer in *Up Pompeii*: 'Woe, woe and thrice woe!' Or hear the people at your neighbourhood barbecue, keening like widows at an African funeral – 'I earn $150,000 but I don't feel rich.' Forget the mining tax; you could raise more with a whining tax.

Can we try to set this collective moaning against a few facts?

We live longer than anyone else on the planet, save for people in Japan and Iceland (and they have to live in Japan and Iceland).

Our two biggest cities, Melbourne and Sydney, regularly feature in the top five for the most liveable cities in the world. (A recent survey, from the Economist Intelligence Unit, rated 140 cities around the world, placing Melbourne first, Sydney sixth and Perth and Adelaide joint eighth.)

In terms of our own incomes, the Bureau of Statistics calculates that, during the past five years, our household incomes have grown faster than inflation, our savings rate is up, and the proportion of our income spent on petrol is actually lower (3.09 per cent of household spending, down from 3.36 per cent).

So much for the hysteria.

We've also become adept at running ourselves down. We routinely talk about Australian men as if they are a tribe of bogans – unable to show emotion, intellectually crippled and obsessed with sport to the exclusion of everything else.

This is not my experience.

If you want a stereotype of an Australian man, I'd say: 'family focused, loyal like a dog, cries at the drop of a hat'. And, okay, obsessed with sport to the exclusion of everything else.

There's also a companion image of the Australian woman as a put-upon doormat, all trackie daks and bedraggled hair: the 'Sheila' to go with the 'Bruce'. I don't claim to know every woman in the country, but the ones I'm familiar with are strong, bordering on stroppy. They are heart-thumpingly attractive, hilarious after two drinks, and do their men the favour of always refusing to take any crap.

A third stereotype: all our teenage children are awful. Why do we say this? I plead guilty myself. We roll our eyes in sympathy with other parents and say: 'I know, aren't they terrible? Mine are a worry, too.' And yet – with a few exceptions and the occasional rocky patch – we all know the truth: this is the best generation of young Australians we've ever seen – smarter, happier and more accepting of difference than we ever were.

So, just now and then, could we take pleasure in what we have?

A beautiful country, shared – aside from the media-induced whingeing – with the smart, sophisticated, hardworking and *lucky* people called Australians.

The Soil and the Seed

A couple of years ago I purchased two massive china pots and installed them on each side of the back door. I filled both with wheelbarrow loads of sweet-smelling compost and planted four gardenia seedlings in each. The pot on the left now offers a profusion of foliage, a tangle of branches bristling with life, while the pot on the right has a few struggling stems and some stunted, lonely leaves looking ready to die.

The way the sun angles in under the veranda roof has created slightly different conditions for the two pots. They're only half a metre apart but the result is dramatic: Garden of Eden on one side; nuclear winter on the other.

They say Australians are obsessed with real estate, and maybe it's true. Deep in our national story there's the idea that the most important thing is 'position, position, position'.

Australia's European history begins in 1788 with the dumping of the human detritus of Britain: people who were poor, mostly ill-educated, criminal. Even in the world before genetics, the First Fleeters were the ultimate example of what would have been called 'bad stock'. Yet, repositioned in the sunlight, they flourished. Given proper conditions, the most seemingly miserable of people could grow tall and true. In the young colony many did so almost instantly, as if the First Fleet were a nursery of struggling and misshapen plants that just needed a splash of water and a shaft of sunlight to come good.

This was Australia's first big discovery: the soil is more important than the seed. Add it to the list that later included Vegemite, the medical use of penicillin, the Hills Hoist and the bionic ear.

To some degree, all of us struggle or flourish according to where we are positioned. Our lives can be hard or easy depending on where the pot is placed. More remarkably, the real estate mantra – position, position, position – can even change the way we feel and behave from day to day.

Most of us, I think, have had this experience: behaving quite differently according to the people in the room at the time. With some people we feel in perpetual shadow; with others, the sunlight seems to angle in and we are aglow.

'What must Warren Whatchamacallit think of me,' you wonder after yet another night in which you were dull, tongue-tied or anxious, letting the discussion whirl around you without taking part. If only you could explain: 'I'm only like this, Warren, when I'm with you. With other people I can be quite good fun.'

With one friend you feel as if you are quite intelligent, discussing complex issues of politics or literature. You are witty, insightful; the right phrase springs to mind at the right time. The very next night, in the company of someone else, you feel dumb and boring. Anxiety or insecurity grips so strongly that the right word, the witty phrase, can never fight its way to the surface.

Even worse can be the experience of visiting your parents in the company of a friend. Suddenly your sunny self disappears and you find yourself transformed into the grunting, sullen fifteen-year-old of ten years before, locked in a dysfunctional relationship with your mother or father or older sister. On your way out the door, you half-wish your friend would reassure your family: 'You know, when you're not around, he's not like this at all. He's actually quite normal.'

I've been thinking about the subtleties of positioning – how the sunlight can hit us when we are standing on this spot but not in this other spot – since a conversation last week. A group of fifty-somethings and twenty-somethings had been talking about the notion of one's 'best self'. Your 'best self' is that self who is open and interested, sometimes entertaining, sometimes erudite, sometimes caring. The 'best self" is the person that reflects your own sense of who you want to be.

The question asked was: with which people are you your best self? And with which your worst self? The discussion was long and revealing, but one moment stood out. One 25-year-old man said to his fifty-something 'aunty': 'I think I'm my best self, or at least my funniest self, when I'm with you.'

Overwhelmed, the aunty – best friend of the boy's mother – found tears in her eyes. That's hardly surprising. The best compliment you can pay someone is to say, 'I like the person I am when I'm with you.'

Personalities form early: that is true. We are a product of our genes: also true. The position of the pot, though, makes such a difference.

Why, then, don't we strive harder to move into the sun? Why don't we spend more time with those who bring out our best selves, and less with those who bring a nuclear winter? Perhaps we could all send out the mental note: 'Warren Whatchamacallit, I know I'm booked in for a barbecue with you on Saturday week but suddenly I find that I am busy. I'm off to spend time with people who think I'm fabulous. And guess what? When I'm with them, I mostly prove them right.'

Acknowledgements

Thanks to all the people who've come to see *Thank God It's Friday* in its various forms and whose laughter, or lack of it, has helped determine the final form of many of these stories. Similarly people who've responded, via Twitter, email, Facebook and the odd brick through the window to my columns in *The Sydney Morning Herald* and *The Age*. I'd like to thank the people I work with at the ABC – in particular Laura Bailey, Sarah McVeigh, Emma Crowe, Renee Krosch and Elizabeth Green – and at the *Herald*'s *Spectrum* section, in particular Gabriel Wilder, Louise Schwartzkoff and John Saxby. At HarperCollins I've had the good fortune to work again with Mary Rennie, Shona Martyn and Anna Valdinger.

My greatest debt, as always, is to my partner, Debra Oswald, a version of whom appears in these pages under the name of Jocasta. Apart from her qualities as a person – the real Debra is much nicer than Jocasta – she constantly takes time from her own writing to make mine better: reading, advising and sometimes laughing (but usually at my spelling).

I try to return the favour. In the last few years Debra's been busy as the creator and head writer of the television drama *Offspring*, and she'll often ask for my help to work out the storyline for an episode. We'll take the dog for a walk and she'll start outlining the various possibilities, correcting herself as she goes, saying, 'No, I think that's wrong for Billie,' or 'Nina wouldn't react like that,' or 'I wonder what would happen if ...'

Occasionally, I nod, or say 'Hmm,' or pick up dog poo, while this river of ideas gushes forth, until – about half an hour later – she talks herself into a breakthrough, and the plot is delivered, all wriggling and shiny and perfect like one of *Offspring*'s babies.

At this point, she'll turn to me, quite serious and intense, and say: 'Thanks for all your help with that, it was so useful.'

And I always reply: 'It was nothing.'

I should mention that her contribution to my work is, in complete contrast, quite significant.

Desperate Husbands

Revisit Richard, the original desperate husband, and his partner, the fabulous but formidable Jocasta. And say hello to their teenage offspring – the Teutonic Batboy and his irrepressible younger brother, The Space Cadet. *Desperate Husbands* lifts the lid on so-called normal family life, and reveals its soulful, hilarious absurdity. Welcome to a world where household appliances conspire against their owners, fathers practise ballet in the hallway, and dead insects spell out an SOS on the kitchen floor.

'Desperate Husbands *is desperately, wickedly funny. I devoured it in one sitting, greedily checking ahead to see that I still had pages left. Richard Glover has done the miraculous – he's made ordinary family life extraordinarily entertaining. This is a must-read for anybody who's ever had a wife or a husband or a mother or a stove or a child or a pulse. Go ahead and open a page at random – you'll laugh out loud.'*
– Augusten Burroughs,
bestselling author of *Running with Scissors*

The Mud House

Four friends, one block of land, no power tools

'One day,' Philip said, 'I'd like to build something bigger ... like a house. We could just buy a block of land, you know, the four of us, and have a go.'

It was just an idea. Then it started to take shape.

'Imagine this – with mud brick you have a building that is made out of the very earth it stands on ... There is another thing: the stuff is free. Once we buy the land we'll have no money left. This way we can get started as soon as we have the block.'

It was a huge and exhausting undertaking by Richard Glover, his friend Philip Clark and their partners. In the end it took them three years of weekend work just to make the bricks. But the process gave Richard the opportunity to examine things he had never quite reconciled to himself – big things like what it means to be a man, the nature of male relationships, fatherhood. It also challenged him in the kind of blokey environment he had previously rejected.

Above all, the mud house proved that even if you don't end up with 'the ceiling of the Sistine Chapel', there is nothing like the satisfaction of making something with your own hands.

Why Men Are Necessary

Wickedly funny stories of everyday life, as heard on ABC Radio's *Thank God It's Friday*. Salute the sexy and feisty Jocasta; confront teenage rebellion in the form of a fish called Wanda; do battle with magpies the size of small fighter jets; try to work out which font you use when speaking the language of love; and find out what men really have to offer.

In Richard Glover's stories, the day-to-day becomes vivid, magical and laugh-out-loud funny.

'Glover is better than Proust. OK, maybe not better, but how often do you find yourself in a cold bath at midnight still chuckling over Proust?'
– Deborah Adelaide